T0247570

HENDO

THE AMERICAN ATHLETE

DAN HENDERSON

WITH DAVID KANO

PERMUTED
PRESS

A PERMUTED PRESS BOOK
ISBN: 978-1-63758-868-0
ISBN (eBook): 978-1-63758-869-7

Hendo:
The American Athlete

Cover photo by Eric Williams / @ewillphoto
Cover design by Franck Ndjamen / @franckjmn
Back cover photo by James Morrey

This is a work of nonfiction. All people, locations, events, and situation are portrayed to the best of the author's memory.

PERMUTED
PRESS

Permuted Press, LLC
New York • Nashville
permutedpress.com

Published in the United States of America

2 3 4 5 6 7 8 9 10

To my dad, Bill Henderson.

Thank you for all of the sacrifices and support. Without your guidance and mental attitude, I would not have accomplished any of the achievements that made me the American athlete!

CONTENTS

FOREWORD

Dan Henderson and I have been friends since 1992. He made the Greco Olympic team that summer, and I managed to come up short again.

Danny and I roomed together on several international tours and championships over the years wrestling for the USA. At first glance, Dan is a reasonably unassuming person, that is until you see him step into the zone of competition. To say he's talented just doesn't begin to cover it. Talent is almost a dirty word. Talented people tend to get away with not putting in as much effort and work as others who are, well, less talented! That was never the case with Dan. For as much talent and experience as Dan possessed, he matched that with his willingness to put in work, whether that be on the mat or in the cage.

I believe that work ethic is what separated Dan "Hollywood" Henderson from the rest of the pack in both the sport of wrestling and MMA. You might not recognize that original nickname "Hollywood" or the small jab at Dan by me for mentioning it. You see, Dan and I both started fighting in the spring of 1997. I signed on with the UFC for UFC 13, and Danny travelled to Brazil for a Vale Tudo competition. Rico and Lou Chiapparelli were managing our careers in this early stage, and Lou and Rico started calling Danny "Hollywood." It was very tongue-in-cheek because if you know Dan, he's anything but Hollywood. In fact, he's usually found in a pair of flip flops, shorts, and a tank top. He's about as laid back as a human can get. He hated that nickname, and that made it stick all the more. Whether you call him Hendo or risk feeling an H-bomb and call him Hollywood, you will never find a more humble, hard-working, and exciting athlete on the planet. His dry sense of humor will catch you off guard and keep you on your toes, and his tenacious warrior spirit will keep you rooting for him to the end, win, lose, or draw.

I'm very excited to present to you Dan's perspective on his journey through life and athletics. I hope you enjoy this book as much as I have.

Thanks Danny for allowing me the honor of contributing to your book with this foreword, for being part of your team, and for all the years of amazing friendship and camaraderie! The journey has been as remarkable as you are, brother.

Randy Couture

★ ★ ☆

PROLOGUE

Plenty of times in my life, I haven't gotten what I wanted. In fact, most times it felt like I had to work my ass off just to get half of what I was aiming for. Maybe even less. I'm not complaining, and I'm thankful for everything I ever managed to accomplish. I have learned a lot of lessons in this life, and all that struggling and grinding has taught me to never give up. If I thought I had one more breath in me, then I would take two. If my opponent took an extra step, so would I. This time, though, what I wanted was a chance to prove I could beat one of the all-time greats. Just like everything else in my life, it wasn't going to come easy. In fact, it was like begging for a chance to street fight a grizzly bear.

The Fedor fight hadn't even been on my radar. When the fight was offered to me, I expressed interest in fighting him not long after I had signed with MMA promotion Strikeforce. I wanted the chance to fight the Russian native who'd been dominating Pride and had gone undefeated in the heavyweight division for over ten years. The opponents he'd defeated were an impressive list of champions, household names, and favorites of the MMA world. Mixed martial arts fans around the globe knew who Fedor "The Last Emperor" Emelianenko was, and they knew his reputation for demolishing almost everyone who had ever stepped into the ring with him. The trouble was, all of this had been done overseas in Pride, Japan's premier fighting promotion. As that organization's top fighter, he was unable to leave to fight for the UFC, which had surpassed Pride years earlier to become the world's MMA leader. The UFC, at that point, had long been the present, and future, of mixed martial arts, and Pride was the past. UFC had purchased Pride in 2007, and they had been in talks with Fedor to get him into their outfit. They had been going on for years and talks had stalled. He took a deal with Strikeforce instead, and I was close to facing the mythological.

I had signed a four-fight deal with Strikeforce, and when I became champion for their promotion, they called for a match between me and Fedor. Much like our shared years in Pride, there was just one problem. We were in different weight classes, and I would have to drink gallons of water to put on weight for the 206-pound minimum for heavyweight. I liked going into the fight the smaller guy, the underdog that wasn't supposed to win. I maintained my strict, disciplined pre-fight regimen of wrestling, striking, and jiu-jitsu, but I also mentally prepped myself to take on Goliath. Fedor was the bigger man physically, and I trained my ass off to take down the MMA great. Not that a size difference has ever been a deterrent to me anyway; I had beaten all five of my opponents in Rings: King of Kings years earlier, and many of those guys had been more than thirty pounds heavier than me.

I think maybe my whole life, I have been the one underestimated. I certainly was in my family. Now, I know I am hardly considered small at 5'11", 200 pounds, but growing up in my household, I think I always took a backseat to my brother's natural talent. Tom was a couple years older than me, and he was an animal. He was faster, stronger, tougher, more aggressive, and angrier. My dad would agree, as would our wrestling coach, the legend Bob Anderson. Everyone thought my brother would be the dominant champion, and maybe I was just a tagalong. Tom was just different from other kids his age and bulldozed through everyone as if he was a grown man fighting children. I always tried to keep up with him and to challenge him where I could, but the reality was he was just better, like older brothers sometimes are.

I had to fight, grind, and struggle for everything I got in this life, and persevere when no one else thought I could make it. Nothing ever came easy, but I think if I have one thing that makes me special, it's that I never quit. I will continue to move forward, chin down, hands up, and keep grinding away until I get where I want to be or get knocked down. Best believe I will be getting back up, though, and then I am going to come at you again. And keep coming. My brother may have had that natural talent as a grappler, but I had the will, the perseverance, and the determination. I wasn't the best at a lot of things in my life, but I was going to try, practice, and execute harder than anyone else until I won or lost.

Going into this Fedor fight felt like business as usual to me. I was training hard, knew what I was going to do, and was just waiting for my turn to put it all on the line. To everyone else, though, I might as well have been preparing for my own funeral. I am sure my friends and family had worried about me fighting before, but never was it more apparent than in the days and weeks leading up to this match. No one would come out and say it, but they were scared, and I could see it on their faces. Fedor Emelianenko was a beast of a man, and he had crushed competitors far larger and maybe even more skilled than me. There was so much weight to his name and his reputation, and it made an impression on those around me. I had never let that fear rule me, though, and I certainly wasn't going to start now. Maybe I should've been scared, but I knew I had what it takes.

I would finally get what I wanted at the end of July in 2011, at the Sears Centre just outside of Chicago, Illinois. Referee Herb Dean brought us to the center of the ring, in front of a cheering crowd and the bright lights of the arena. Standing face-to-face with Fedor, I thought we matched up well. But when the announcer was introducing us, I looked up at the tale of the tape and saw he had a two-inch reach advantage and thought, *Oh shit, he's longer than I thought, but it won't matter.* Herb Dean explained the rules while Fedor and I rocked back and forth, waiting for the fight to start. Neither of us postured or tried to intimidate the other. I respected that about him. He knew who he was, and he didn't have to try and out-tough-guy me before the fight. Same with me. We would let our fists do all the talking shortly.

"Gentleman, touch gloves."

Our fists met in center ring, and I backed off immediately to my corner. Fedor did the same. Herb Dean yelled, "Fight," and I started to push hard towards Fedor. We touched gloves one more time, and then I was almost shocked as Fedor immediately threw a double left jab while I threw a kick simultaneously. *Holy shit, this is happening.* He followed with a right hook that I ducked while throwing an overhand right of my own. He slipped under it with ease. He was quicker than I thought, but I caught him with a powerful left hook that stunned him, and at that moment he knew that the little guy could hit hard too. We clinched and I smashed into him with a knee to his chest while trying to get an underhook in. I pushed forward with all of my strength and momentum, but it was like trying to move a bear. *Oh shit, I'm getting spun into the cage.* I dipped out and missed a big shot coming straight for my head. Lucky for me. I moved back to the center of the ring, and we both started right back toward each other. This fucker was big—and hit hard. Nothing had connected too flush yet, but it was coming. We both let loose and started throwing big shots. Someone was gonna go down in this flurry.

I took a shotgun blast of an overhand right square to the face. Emelianenko was rushing forward hard, sensing that punch had hurt me, but I wasn't fazed. I moved, trying with everything I had to defend myself from a flurry of punches delivered *Rocky IV* style via The Last Emperor. I needed to stay on my feet. My hands were up, trying desperately to block each punch, but they were making their way through. All 220-plus pounds behind his six-foot frame were charging at me, and he connected with a short left, then another, followed by the snap of a right, and finished with a lightning-quick left hook. The punches put me off balance, and before I knew what was happening, I was on my ass. I had been caught off guard, but now was going to endure a flurry. Fedor closed the distance and was on top of me before I had time to think or breathe. I was going to have to dig deep and keep my head and wits about me, like I'd done countless times before. I bit down on my mouthpiece, and his fist was screaming down toward my face as he looked to end it....

☆☆☆

1

PUT A BAND-AID ON IT

"Hey, Dad, can I go play out back?"

It was a Sunday afternoon, and my dad and grandpa were glued to the television. Sunday in the fall meant football. My dad rarely watched television—he'd rather be doing something with his hands—but their favorite team, the Los Angeles Rams, was on, and my dad was fine to give me a day off of training.

"Yes, you can go outside."

I was five years old and didn't care about football since I wasn't a part of it. I always seemed to be energetic and wanted to be active. Who had time to watch TV? Heck, I'd rather play by myself. It was 1975 and there were no smartphones, iPhones, tablets, social media, or billions of apps for us to get addicted to. No YouTube, no PlayStation, no Xbox, no Nintendo, no Netflix, no nothing. I didn't have to worry about the countless television shows or millions of hours of content to watch, all of which would be meaningless. We had sports, toys, and our imaginations.

I headed outside by myself because my mom and older brother, Tom, weren't home. Our backyard was filled with various things to play with. Some toys here, balls there, wood planks, tools, cinderblocks—if you wanted to play back there or make something, you could. Looking for circuit training or an obstacle course? We had that too. Want to build a steel submarine? We probably had everything needed in the shed or garage, but on that particular day, I just wanted to play.

When I walked outside, I grabbed my leather baseball glove and ball and started to play catch with myself. I'd throw the ball in the air as hard as I could and catch it on the way down. Each time I would try to throw it harder and farther in the air. *Plop, plop, plop.* Ah, the sound of the ball hitting the mitt. I had a pretty good arm, and I was always pushing to see if I could maybe hit the sun with the ball. I never succeeded, but I tried nonetheless.

I got bored tossing the ball and was looking around for things to do. Being a kid, I liked to climb, and the brick walls along the side of the house were just asking to be scaled. One of those walls had my number that day, though, and while making my climb, I slipped and lost my footing. I fell backwards near one of the piles of cinderblocks and caught the inside of my arm under my elbow on a jagged edge. It opened me up a couple inches along my arm, deep too. I didn't see the massive block—they were spread out and stacked or piled haphazardly in our backyard, and now I had blood gushing out. *Oh shit.* It hurt a little bit and stung when I touched it so I headed inside because it didn't look good. To this day, I can't exactly remember how big that cut was, but I know it was pretty long and pretty deep. I could fit a few kid-sized fingers in it, and even at five I knew I shouldn't be able to see raw flesh inside of my arm. I headed inside and went to the living room.

"Dad."

"What is it, Dan?"

"Um. I fell down."

"Okay."

"Dad, I cut my arm."

My dad turned from his chair to take a quick look. It was bloodied up, and I hadn't figured out how to stop the bleeding yet. If my mom was home, I would've headed straight to her. She'd know how to fix it. But it was my dad, who was over six feet tall, weighing around 230 pounds of pure muscle and a former collegiate wrestler and Mr. Natural California. It was like telling Superman I had a scratch. Except this wasn't small.

"Go put a band-aid on it."

That was it. There wouldn't be any further discussion. What my dad said was final, so I went to our bathroom and looked for a band-aid but couldn't find one. I washed off my arm, but the blood was still pouring out.

"Dad. No band-aids." My dad didn't even turn around. "Go next door."

Superman, er, my dad, didn't seem too concerned, so I headed to our next-door neighbor's house to ask for a band-aid. The neighbor's wife opened the door, and after I showed her my cut, she rushed me in and cleaned out my arm, put some Vaseline and gauze on it to stop the bleeding, and bandaged it up. It still hurt a little bit, but at least the bleeding stopped. I went back to my house and headed to my backyard once again.

The generation I was brought up in seems like they were from a whole other planet than the one we're on today. If this happened to one of my kids, I'd at least look at the cut before telling 'em to go put a fuckin' band-aid on it. To this day I have this scar, and stitches probably wouldn't have made it any better. This generation is softer. All that progress, I guess. Yeah, there are still some tough kids out there, but back when I was growing up *most* kids were tough. Now they're few and far between. They don't have that same grit and determination to get through pain or tough times. It seems like it takes a little bit longer for them to figure that out.

I was born August 24, 1970, in Downey, California. It's a suburb of Los Angeles County, and I lived close by in Whittier until third grade. Going into fourth grade, my parents moved to Apple Valley, which is about ninety minutes north and known as the Victorville area of San Bernardino County. We were able to get a house with a bigger yard, and it was a bit quieter than Whittier. I spent the rest of my adolescence there, and, even though it's not a place known for its heralded athletes, my dad intended I be one no matter where we ended up. You'll find out my father didn't worry about what others did, where they did it, or how. He had a plan for his sons, and his own life and work ethic was the blueprint. It was how hard we could work, how far we could be pushed.

Looking back, I don't know if my dad was trying to toughen me up, he just was like that—this is how things were done at my house. It was like he was teaching me, "don't be crying about little things." As a kid, you always want to whine to mom but better make sure you don't go to dad. He would have none of it. I think he expected more from us, and that made us expect more from ourselves. I know it did for me. And this stuck with me and my brother. We didn't cry about the little things.

About a year after my arm fiasco, my parents had left me and my brother alone at the house. After we finished our chores, we were free to play. I could have fun and entertain myself alone, but having an older brother made it that much better—and more competitive. That day we decided to play tag. Instead of just chasing Tom, I grabbed a Los Angeles Rams football helmet to put on.

My dad had brought the helmet home one day after working out. His gym was one of those hole-in-the-wall places where people go to lift, work out, and get out. Not the corporate gyms of today with the thousand television screens, filtered water fountains, or senior citizen aqua classes. Nothing wrong with any of those amenities, but my dad was just about work and results. He was always laser focused (one of the many traits I would pick up from him) and didn't have time to waste.

There was a reason someone had thrown the Rams helmet to the wayside. It was missing all of the padding inside, and when I put it on, the helmet had this hard, sharp plastic on the inside and no protection from any impact. It also felt twenty sizes too big for me and was loose, even with the strap on.

"Alright, Dan, you ready?" my brother said.

"Yup, let's go."

With that, Tom was off running. I started chasing him, but he was fast. I was fast too, but that year and a half of muscle development he had on me gave him a greater advantage. I was close on his heels, though, and when he cut sharply to the left, I was right there. He ran through the kitchen to take a hard turn to his right, but I was gaining on him. He sprinted to one of the bedrooms; it was a straightaway, and I knew it was my chance to tag him. He knew it too, and we both ran full speed. As soon as he got inside the room, he slammed the door shut just as I was about to get him, and the door smashed into my loose, padless helmet. The impact swiveled the helmet around like a can opener and cut my head open, just above my eyebrow. *Damn, not again.* Once again, I'd sliced myself open. The crash of the helmet hitting the door was sickeningly loud, and me not pursuing Tom anymore must've alerted him the game was over. When he finally opened it, he saw the blood dripping. A lot of blood.

"Shit. Let's put something on it."

We headed to the bathroom and grabbed a washcloth, put some water on it, and I held it to my head. I remembered from my arm being cut that pressure would stop the blood, and Tom and I took turns holding it until my parents came home. I was always up for a good game, but the fun was over for now. It was time to see what Mom and Dad had to say.

They came home soon after and were surprised. Not because I had cut myself open or because we were playing with a busted football helmet, but impressed we had the wherewithal to put a washcloth on it and wait for them. I wasn't freaked out about the cut and was glad we didn't get in any trouble, but the cut needed stitches, and my parents took me in to the doctor's where they numbed it up and stitched it. I guess they thought, we were boys just being boys.

As boys, we knew what we could get away with—and the consequences if we were out of line. Mom and Dad both spanked us, but there was a drastic difference in their methodology. When mom gave us a whooping, it didn't hurt much and didn't deter us from whatever it was we had been doing. If my dad did the disciplining, it was as if the sun stood still. Time would stop. There would be nothing nice nor gentle when me and my brother screwed up. Iron Man couldn't stop my dad. I was convinced my dad had superhero strength every time I'd get a spanking from him. You wouldn't wish his spankings on your worst enemy.

Here was the thing. My dad didn't know his own strength. He truly didn't. He would buy bulk steel and use a welding torch to make his own weights by hand. The man was a wrestler, bodybuilder, and high school physical education teacher. He was always doing something. And when it was time for us to get spanked, he would grab whatever board was around to whack us. These weren't paddles made for a good swat; he would grab two-by-fours or picture-frame molding. Since he was always making something, there was never a shortage of lumber.

The two-by-fours seem egregious, but they didn't hurt nearly as bad as the picture-frame molding. The two-by-four planks were wider, so at least there was more surface area for my butt to absorb the blow, but the thin, sturdy, strong molding was a whole other story.

My dad would make his own picture frames, and most don't realize the molding used in the real wood frames are nearly unbreakable. It felt like a leather bullwhip made of wood. I don't know what a bullwhip feels like, but I'd imagine the feeling to be similar if you swapped out the cowhide for wood.

What my mom couldn't deter us from, my dad certainly was able to correct. I didn't make the same mistake twice when he got ahold of me. I knew if I did, there would be dire repercussions from the real-life "Man of Steel." It may sound horrific by today's standards, but it was good for me. It helped redirect my negative actions and instilled discipline and respect. It also showed me that bad behavior had consequences. He didn't injure me, and I wasn't one of those kids covered in bruises. It was painful, sure, but I wasn't brutally beaten either.

Looking around my yard at all of the wood and possible butt-smacking items lying around while waiting for my dad to get home from work after I fucked up was the worst. It was the fear of the punishment that was effective. Much different from today, where parents use timeouts as a deterrence or try talking to their kids in hopes of changing their behavior. It seemed like what my dad did worked, at least on me.

"Tom, Dan, let's go."

I was in kindergarten still learning my ABCs and how to write my name, but it was time to head to wrestling practice with my brother. My dad had put me and Tom in a wrestling club the same time I started grade school. After school we would head to West

Covina two to three times a week, where I was learning single-leg takedowns, double-leg takedowns, ankle laces, crotch lifts, takedown defense, and ankle picks. And I had to make damn sure I didn't get pinned. I loved competing, even at five, and was eager to learn on the mats.

"Dan, what are you doing? Grab his leg and turn him the other way!"

Even though my dad wasn't the head coach, he would still help out and teach me and the other kids on the team. When our club headed to wrestling tournaments on the weekend, if I screwed up, I'd hear his voice in my head. When I didn't do a technique right, I'd see my dad get rigid and tense up.

As I started to learn the moves, I knew when my head was in the wrong position. *Ah, shit. Why did I do it like that?!* Not transition properly from a double-leg to a single? *Come on, Dan! Do it right!* Dad's voice quickly became my own. I was a fast learner, but as a five-year-old still developing my gross and fine motor skills, drilling constantly was the only way to get the moves and technique down. I wasn't a super freak athlete or a mini Superman. I was on the mats having fun rolling around, but at the same time trying to soak in what was being taught.

My dad's wrestling career had ended just a couple years before I was born. He had wrestled in high school, and then moved on to Cerritos College in Southern California. He was a solid wrestler in his own right. While at Cerritos, he won state in his weight class and transferred to California State University Long Beach to wrestle. But that's where it stopped. Long Beach discontinued their wrestling program the year he transferred in. My brother was already born, and I came along while he was finishing up his teaching degree at Long Beach. With a wife and two kids, a toddler and a baby, my dad had decided to get his teaching credential and let wrestling go. It was the 1970s, and there was no money in wrestling. Hell, there's hardly any money in it today either, but back then our family of four would've been on the streets if wrestling was his career. Even the entertainment wrestlers on television weren't making much.

My dad was always a provider first and foremost and chose to get a teaching job right after college. Not that teaching was a huge payday, but he was able to provide for us. We weren't rich, but we certainly weren't poor. He may have had to give up his passion, but he was able to pass it down to me and Tom.

By third grade I had figured out the writing-words-in-cursive thing, addition, subtraction, and other basic shit. Multiplication and division were something else entirely, though, and school was just school to me. That same year my dad took over as head wrestling coach in our club.

I was constantly improving my moves, technique, and positioning, which my dad had a big influence on. As a high school teacher, he was able to read students, and as a coach, he was able to observe where I was at and what I needed to improve upon. A year after he took over, we started making the drive to the national wrestling tournament in Nebraska.

I was eight years old when I first competed in nationals, and the competition there was a step up from the local kids in Southern California. There were some good wrestlers in my area, but I would compete against kids from Pennsylvania, Iowa, Ohio—big, strong farm kids who probably started wrestling in their barnyard before they could first walk. It was a wake-up call for me, but it broadened my understanding of the sport and where I stood in it.

The first time we returned from nationals, I could tell the experience had made me better. I never won a tournament, but during my elementary school years, I placed in the top three once or twice. And, at that time, I didn't eat, breathe, or sleep wrestling like some have assumed. My parents still let me do regular kid stuff. They had me enrolled in America's Pastime, baseball, a sport far different from wrestling but one that I enjoyed playing. Long before the H-Bomb was knocking people out and sending them to the floor, I had a strong arm. I played pitcher, catcher, and third base, all positions that required having an arm that could laser-beam a ball to its intended target. *Splat!* I loved the sound of a ball hitting the catcher's mitt when I was pitching. *Whoosh!* Catching the ball and hearing it as I threw someone out at second base. *Fwoop!* Digging in and getting the ground ball at third and firing it as hard as I could to the first baseman and hearing, "You're out!" was a gratifying feeling. I loved *competing*. That's what I liked most about playing sports. And winning was *always* far better than losing. So why not try to win? Every time. Go out and give it my all.

"Alright, boys, pack your gear and let's go."

When my dad said to do something, you just did it. The boundaries were pretty clear with that guy. Me and Tom put our wrestling gear in our bag, got in the car, and picked up four of our wrestling teammates. My dad didn't say why, and we headed off to a place that seemed as far away as Nebraska.

After a two-hour car ride, we ended up in Camp Pendleton. It's the northernmost tip of San Diego County and has been home to the largest Marine Corp base in the United States since 1942. I was in fifth grade when my training at the base started. At ten, I was too young to be a Marine, but not too young to train with another badass wrestler and superhero, Bob Anderson.

If my dad was Superman, then Bob was The Incredible Hulk. Bob was a wrestling state champion, a NCAA All-American in college, who wrestled in the 1968 Olympic Trials and was a two-time gold medalist at the Pan American Championships. If that wasn't enough, he competed in Sambo, trained with the legendary Rolls Gracie (whose father, Carlos Gracie, was the founder of

Brazilian jiu-jitsu with his brother Hélio Gracie) and taught Rolls the Americana, which was later named after him.

Rolls had never seen the move performed before—some called it a keylock—where you bend your opponent's arm in an *L* shape and crank it until they tap or risk breaking, dislocating, or otherwise tearing the arm up. If those accolades weren't enough, throughout his career he would go on to coach Olympic gold medalist Rulon Gardner (who had one of the biggest upsets in wrestling history), Olympian Heath Sims, and UFC champion Randy Couture. I would also be lucky enough to have him be one of my coaches on the 1996 Olympic team.

At the age of sixty, Bob would decide to compete once again and, at the 2003 World Masters, took first place in his division. Let's just say if it wasn't for my dad and Bob, Dan Henderson wouldn't be who he is today.

"Can I help you?"

We had pulled up to the military base, and a guy dressed in fatigues with a gun started to question my dad. I could see there was a gate arm closed and had no idea why we were here.

"Yes, my sons are here for the wrestling camp with Bob Anderson."

"Okay, sir, thank you. Go ahead and drive straight until you hit the Quonset huts."

Quanta what? I was really confused as to why we'd come to a Marine base to wrestle. And what the heck were these huts? We pulled up to the Quonset huts, which were these half cylindrical barracks that looked like an airplane with no wings that was cut through the middle. There were other parents with their kids that started showing up on that Friday evening. I recognized some of them as the best ones I had competed against in my wrestling tournaments. What were they doing here?

The six of us barreled out of my dad's old-school Ford Econoline 150. It was like a tank and hotel, all in one. We went everywhere in that thing. And, on long trips, there was so much space, we were able to sleep on the bed or couch that it had in the back. I doubt it would be close to passing emissions today, but the wrestling-mobile did its job back then.

"Alright, I'll be back to pick you all up on Sunday." With that, my dad left.

Well, I guess I'm spending the night here, I thought. Bob brought us to one of the three Quonset huts designated for us. Two of them were for the kids, and the other was for the coaches. It was kind of cool. I'd be sleeping in a cot and quarters where Marines had been. And, I figured, I was there to wrestle. To *compete*. This wasn't so bad.

After I threw my gear on one of the cots, we were told to head to chow hall, which was a two-mile trek away from the huts. By the time we finished eating, it was almost 7:00 p.m., and we headed to the gym for wrestling practice. I was one of the younger kids in the group, which ranged from fifth to eighth grade. There were only a few faces I recognized—everyone else was new to me. When we started to practice, there was a heightened intensity compared to my club in Victorville. It was like the air was different.

After practice, we showered and headed to our huts, and the coaches made sure lights were out by ten. On Saturday, we woke up at 6:30 a.m., and after brushing our teeth, had to jog the two miles to chow hall instead of walking. As we were jogging, we would hear the Marines chanting and would mimic their sayings. It was like we were one of them. Soldiers fighting for our country, but we were just fighting to be better wrestlers.

After breakfast we were allowed to walk back to the barracks, and our first practice would start at ten and go for a couple hours. We would shower, head to chow hall again and eat lunch, then relax until 3:30 when we had another training session. That practice would last a minimum of two and a half hours, depending on how hard Bob and the coaches wanted to push us, then we would go back to the barracks and shower. We would go to chow hall for dinner, then lift weights for an hour, shower, and go back to the barracks, where my cot became my best friend and I could sleep. I would be exhausted by the time lights went out at ten, and on Sunday, we would do it all over again, except this time, my dad would pick us up after dinner, and we'd make the trip from Camp Pendleton back to Victorville.

This would become my routine every week. No more wrestling against kids that weren't close to my skill level. Now I was wrestling against the best of the best in Southern California. Bob would go to wrestling tournaments from all around the area: Los Angeles County, San Bernardino County, Riverside County, Orange County, and San Diego County to recruit the best kids for his wrestling camp. He'd charge parents nine dollars to house, feed, and train their kids. No profit was taken. Bob didn't do it for the money. He was all about the coaching, wrestling, and maybe, one of the kids would go on to do something great. It was about making these highly talented and motivated kids better. And it worked. Every weekend I would have three or four matches against kids that wanted to beat me just as bad as I wanted to beat them. One of the lessons I learned quickly from Bob was that there were levels to everything in life, and I had gone up another notch. I was now going to progress and get better at a faster rate. I wasn't thinking ahead of winning world championships, I didn't have Olympic grandeur in my sight. I just wanted to beat everyone that was put in front of me. Period.

☆☆☆

2

WARRIOR IN TRAINING

For years when people heard the word "wrestling," they thought about the choreographed and scripted WWE on television. Competitive wrestling is slowly making its way into the mainstream, but for those who have not trained, they think it's all the same. It is a martial art, and without it, most mixed martial artists would never be champion. There are drastically different styles of wrestling, and when you're competing, each one has its own rule set and parameters for winning or losing a match. It's like competing with different rules in jiu-jitsu, Taekwondo, kickboxing, karate, or any other martial art. In America, there are three different types: Greco-Roman wrestling, freestyle wrestling, and folkstyle (also called collegiate wrestling).

There are similarities and differences between the three of them, but the biggest difference between Greco-Roman and freestyle or folkstyle is that in Greco-Roman you cannot attack an opponent's legs or trip them. All throws or takedowns must be done above the waist. That makes it much more difficult to take someone down. And when two people are equally matched up, it's like a chess match because one wrong move and you're down on points.

In freestyle and folkstyle, you can grab your opponent's legs and trip, in addition to throwing from their waist up, but the point system is much different. Different moves mean different points in freestyle, whereas in folkstyle, a highly technical move can get someone the same amount of points as a basic move. There are other nuances between them, but when people ask me, "Which one is the hardest?" I say to just look at the Olympics, the highest level of wrestling. Greco-Roman wrestling has been around since the very first Olympic Games at Athens in 1896. In 1904, freestyle wrestling made its debut in the Olympics, and over one hundred years later, the two of them are still in the Summer Games.

"I'm sure you'll have a good time camping with your family, Johnny. And Dan, what are your family plans for this weekend?"

It was the end of my first week in fifth grade, and my teacher wanted to know what I was going to do. He didn't know me too well, but every time he asked, it would be the same answer every Friday for the whole year.

"I'm going to Camp Pendleton with my dad and brother for wrestling camp."

"Um, okay. Wrestling?" My teacher looked puzzled.

"Yes, wrestling," I said.

"Okay, Dan, well, um, have fun, I guess."

He probably didn't understand, but then again, most people didn't. That was just my life. Wrestling. And training. It was difficult, steadily becoming routine, but fun at the same time.

I may have been an average student, but I was slowly honing my wrestling technique and skills. There were changes at the start of my second year with Bob. My dad didn't just drop us off anymore. He stayed in a Quonset hut with the coaches, and Bob added him to his coaching staff.

During the week, my dad would coach the youth program at Victor Valley High School, and after our practice there, he was an assistant coach for the varsity team. If being a full-time teacher and a wrestling coach for the youth and high schoolers wasn't enough for my dad, he added to his workload by joining Bob's program and club, the California Jets. Unbeknownst to me and my brother, my dad accepted. Their goal was for American wrestlers to be competitive with the rest of the world, but for this to happen, they knew it was vital to start teaching techniques used at the world level to kids from the get-go. If American wrestlers waited until after college to learn and train in the Greco-Roman and Freestyle techniques, we would lag behind the European and Eastern European countries, which would usually dominate at the world level.

Phweeeeeeet! "Line it up."

The whistle meant practice was in session. And with my dad there, it meant extra scrutiny for me. We were about to drill anywhere from ten to twenty moves, fifty times each. The coaches were there to make sure we did it right. And if we didn't, we were damn sure going to hear about it. Not in a condescending way, but a "stop fucking it up" type of way. At twelve, I had to rely on my technique, not strength. I had a skinny, wiry frame—I wasn't close to the muscle or brawn I would have as an adult. Tom, on the other hand, was stronger than everyone in his age group. He would pin kids in tournaments when we were younger and be done for the day. Even when he was with the Jets, he was stronger than the best kids in our region and when we competed at the national level. When we were older and competed in Russia at a dual meet, he would be chosen by the other wrestlers to be the best. I was just trying to get better every day, and when I would get beat, I wanted to know why and what I could've done to win.

At the end of sixth grade, we started staying with Bob for a week at a time and trained with the Jets every day. Part of my dad and Bob's master plan was a weight-training regimen to make us stronger. At home my dad would make me and my brother lift weights on a universal machine in our makeshift gym that he built, but initially, we weren't into lifting. We would sit at our exercise area resting and talking when my dad would leave the garage, but as soon as he got back, we would grab the weights quickly and start moving again like we had been lifting the entire time he was gone. When we trained with Bob, that changed. There was always a coach watching us, and Bob and my dad came out with a new regimen.

In fifth grade we would do a circuit training program of twenty reps per set and exercises going from arms to legs and then legs back to arms. There would be no break, just going from one exercise to another would be our rest time. In sixth grade the reps increased to thirty per set—with the weight increasing as well. Well, the summer going into seventh grade, Bob pushed the reps up to forty per set, and an increase in weight.

What Bob and my dad figured out was that doing more reps per set and a lower weight would not only increase power, but also drastically improve muscle endurance and lead to less injuries. They saw that those who lifted heavier weight and less reps were more prone to muscle injuries like tears and strains to their muscles or ligaments. Their hypothesis was to push the body harder for a longer period of time with decreased weight to have an athlete that could endure much longer. And, in some ways, it really produced results.

The Marines had an obstacle course that we would use as part of our training as well. We would run and scale over walls, crawl on our stomachs underneath a square roped barrier, then have to muster all of our energy to rope climb and touch the top before we could get down. I had been doing that obstacle course for two years, and that's when Bob wanted to pit us against the Marines. I guess he thought we were ready to compete with them, and one day Bob spoke to a drill sergeant.

"Hey, Sergeant."

"Bob, I see your kids getting better."

"They are, but I bet they can beat your boys."

"What?"

"Let's put your best against our best and see who comes out on top."

It didn't matter to Bob. Even though Bob was putting middle schoolers and high schoolers against eighteen-to-twenty-year-old Marines, he believed our training superseded what they were doing, and he was right. Every time we went head-to-head with the Marines, we won. As a seventh grader, I was surprised, but wasn't. We were kids beating young men, but no one was outworking us—and no one was going to outwork me. I wasn't the best yet, but I wouldn't quit. I was going to get better, and in my seventh- and eighth-grade years, things started to change.

If wrestling was my full-time job those elementary and middle school years, then baseball was my part time gig. I loved playing all sports, with the best part being competition, but I had excelled in baseball over the years. But in those last two years of junior high, it started to not be fun anymore. I was getting less playing time, and the less I played the more I lost interest. Plus, the coach's kid played the same position as me, and he got the nod more than I did.

I didn't understand why; I could smack a baseball and throw people out with ease. Maybe it was more about giving everyone a chance, but I didn't get how the better player didn't play. In wrestling, if you won, you moved on. If you lost, you were out. Case closed. Why wasn't it like this in all sports? I suppose if my dad coached baseball, it would've been different. When I told him I didn't want to play baseball anymore, he was fine with it. Besides, deep down, I was a mini warrior, a wrestler. I enjoyed hand-to-hand combat, and baseball, well, it just wasn't that.

In seventh and eighth grade I started to feel a shift inside myself, and my competitiveness started to rise more than it had already. It was like a switch inside of me had slowly been flipped to *on*. I went from this mild-mannered, happy-go-lucky kid who enjoyed learning new wrestling techniques and competing, to a mild-mannered kid who still soaked up new wrestling techniques and loved competing—but now wanted, needed to win every time. Don't get me wrong, I didn't want to lose before, but it didn't matter as much to me. I was out there having a good time, learning how to wrestle, and doing the same thing as my big brother. Now, though, I wanted to perfect the techniques being taught and fix my mistakes.

At that same time, Bob moved the Jets from Camp Pendleton to San Clemente, where he lived. It allowed us to train more days during the year there. The agreement with the colonel at Pendleton only included weekends and summers. On school days off, Christmas break, or spring break, we didn't have access to the base. In San Clemente, though, we were able to train any time, and I mean *any time*. For me and my brother, it was school, chores, wrestling, and weights. And San Clemente also gave us an extra workout. On Sunday mornings, Bob (who is also Christian), would give us thirty-minute messages on the Bible and talk about Jesus Christ dying on the cross for our sins. Following his message, we would go down to the beach, and he would give us a surfboard for our opening workout. He would make us paddle into the waves, along the waves, then back into the shore. We would repeat this for about an hour. Paddling may seem easy, but when you're going headstrong into a wave, you've got to use every ounce of your strength to get over it. If you don't, the wave will push you over and then you've got to deal with another one right behind it. The Pacific Ocean can be unforgiving, and most people who have never battled waves don't really understand how strong water is. All of us would be exhausted by the end of this rigorous workout. Bob, who was an avid surfer, would tell us we could go surf for a bit after the hour of hell in the water. We were so tired, though, there wasn't an ounce of energy left for us to do so.

At the end of training, instead of staying in Quonset huts, we would pack into Bob's house to spend the night. We didn't have the luxury of getting a hotel each weekend, but it didn't matter. We all shared the singular focus of getting better. The coaches were trying to find better techniques and ways to help us excel, and we were growing physically, mentally, and becoming more skilled as the weeks went by.

When we made the long drive to Nebraska for nationals my seventh- and eighth-grade years, I placed in the top five but wasn't able to medal. Simply put, I wasn't the best in my age or weight class yet. I *needed* to get better. When I lost, Bob would see my frustration and just encourage me.

"You did a good job, Danny."

"Yea, thanks, Coach."

"Just keep working at it, Danny. You'll get there. Take it one day at a time, you'll see."

I wanted to win every time. I don't think Bob thought of me as the best one out of the group, but I think he understood how badly I wanted to get better. I was paying more attention to the nuances of each move and learning the counters to the moves I would lose to. Wrestling is like chess; there is always something that can be done to offset your opponent. The question is, can you employ it before it's too late, and if you get countered, what is your next move? As a student of the game, those years I worked at learning those counters as I drilled and trained to be better. High school was up next, and I wanted to be prepared to compete with older kids in my weight class.

It was 1984 when the Summer Olympics came to Los Angeles. I was headed into my freshman year of high school, and I knew all about the Olympics. That's where the best Greco-Roman and free-style wrestlers compete every four years, and I was glad when my dad said we would host families from Sweden and Norway who had family members competing in the Games.

My dad had met them through culture exchange trips where he would take a group of wrestlers to different European countries, and they would stay with these host families who had their sons in their respected national wrestling programs. The goal was to make everyone better in cross training with the different countries. Now that some of them had made it to the Olympics, my dad and Bob were happy to house them for the summer.

I didn't know what to expect when my dad took me to see the athletes compete. We saw some track and field competitions, but it was mainly wrestling. I didn't tell anyone at the time, but it was at that moment that I knew I wanted to represent my country at the Olympics. Being able to see these athletes in their prime going head-to-head was like a composer being able to watch Mozart in his prime. I wanted to be the one to take on the world. I wanted to be an Olympic champion.

I attended Victor Valley High School in Victorville, California, and was like any other high school student. I wasn't a book person, and I mostly got Cs with some Bs sprinkled on my report card. The only A I would get every semester was in physical education, the only subject I was able to master. Wrestling was different in high school as well. I would be doing folkstyle for the school, but the California Interscholastic Federation (CIF), which governs high school sports in California, would not allow me to wrestle or train with the Jets during wrestling season. Since the high school season didn't start until November, I still had a couple months of training with Bob.

My freshman year Bob had rented an industrial warehouse and turned it into our new headquarters. They had installed showers and bathrooms, so instead of spending the night at Bob's house, we brought sleeping bags to sleep in the warehouse on the weekends. Bob had increased our weight training regimen as well. Fifty-rep sets were what they thought would be feasible for us to do. I was still lean and long for my weight class, but my strength had not caught up to the naturally bigger and stronger kids in my division. Where I lacked in power and strength, I made up for in technique and skill, and I was able to beat some of the kids I had lost to before. And if I did lose, that would make me want to train harder. I didn't want someone else to be victorious over me.

When the high school wrestling season started, my dad took on a firmer role as my coach. He was an assistant coach at the high school, and he acted as if he was the judge, jury, and executioner my first year with him there. Bob didn't run practice with an iron fist, but then again, I wasn't his son. Bill Henderson, on the other hand, expected more out of me. If one of my chores didn't get done, I would get more chores added to my workload. I suppose it was because of my dad's upbringing that he had a no-nonsense and tough, hard-working mentality. My grandfather, another Bill Henderson, had polio when he was five years old and needed to wear a leg brace for his entire life. Even with his disability, he would run construction crews and had high expectations for the guys he hired. If there were guys that couldn't keep up with him, he wouldn't hire them back. He figured if they weren't able to hang with a guy who had a bum leg, then they weren't working hard enough and were not cut out to do construction work.

My grandfather employed this same energy towards my father. If my dad didn't get chores done, my grandfather would add extra chores for him to do. And there wasn't a shortage of work on their property. They had cornfields, avocado trees, citrus trees, steers, and who knows what else. This was just a domino effect on me and my brother. The training, practice, and work all needed to be done right.

So when I started wrestling in high school, it was as if my dad leveled up in pushing me. When I didn't do a move to his liking, he would make me do fifty pushups and do the move over. I would think to myself, *What the fuck?!* He wouldn't ride me like that when I was training with Bob; I would just keep drilling to get it done better. And there was no one at my school in my weight class that was at my level. My dad *knew* that. But he still would yell at me. I would see other guys on the team fucking up big time, but he just *coached* them. It was like, since I was his son, he wanted to prove a point and single me out in front of everyone, even when I knew I was doing the move right. It wasn't like I was half-assing anything. It just wasn't the way he liked it. Maybe it was because he knew I wouldn't get the same training during wrestling season until we picked back up with Bob in January that he was extra hard on me. Maybe it was because of my grandfather being tough on him as he came into manhood. Whatever it was, I hated it. It was pissing me off, and I was coming to a breaking point. I needed to vent my frustration, but I would let him know it my own way.

"Dan, get down and do fifty more pushups. Do it right!"

This was the week. We were halfway through the season, and I was done being the scapegoat for no good reason. *Okay, here we go,* I thought to myself. *If he wants me to do fifty pushups every time, I'll really fuck up.*

"Alright, Dan, do it again. Focus!"

I went back to the drill after the pushups and purposely fucked it up.

"What the fuck, Dan, I told you to do it right. Fifty more pushups!"

I got called out to do five hundred pushups that practice. I didn't care, and I did them with gritted teeth. I would fuck up on purpose. The next day, my dad went at me again, and once again, I had a shitty practice doing moves half-ass. I was doing five hundred pushups every practice session until my dad finally got it. He pumped the brakes and stopped riding me for every single thing he didn't like. It was about time too. I wasn't going to explode and attack my dad or anything, but I would have just shut down if it continued. I would have kept doing shit wrong on purpose, but he saw what I was doing and adjusted. He stopped singling me out for small shit and started to yell at other kids for a change. From that point on, we didn't have any more problems.

My first two years in high school, I didn't cut any weight. I wrestled at 119 pounds my freshman year and 138 pounds as a sophomore. After the high school season we would head to San Clemente and resume our Greco-Roman and freestyle training with Bob and the Jets. I didn't place my freshman or sophomore years but learned a vital lesson at junior nationals my sophomore year. One of the kids competing was pinning most of his opponents, and some of us were wondering how he did it. He told us, "Instead of worrying about winning by points, you all need to change your attitude. Fuck the points, pin your opponent."

I always wanted to win. It didn't matter if it was by points or pin. I still wasn't that strong, but my strength was increasing. I hadn't seen the point in lifting weights when I was younger but was beginning to understand the importance of being strong, especially when wrestling against someone of a similar skill level. And I was determined to get much better, but to do that, I had to get meaner.

———————

"Dan, get up and get your shit done, I need you to come to the store with me later."

Even though my parents had house rules, I was like any other high schooler and would go to parties when I wasn't in wrestling season. There were times I wasn't given a curfew and would sometimes stay out all night, but that didn't exclude me from my weekly chores. My dad didn't really care what I did as long as I passed class, trained, and did what I was told around the house. My parents knew I wasn't a troublemaker and didn't bother anyone. I was quiet and reserved with my Olympic dreams in my head, even if no one else thought it was a possibility.

My junior year Bob had increased my weight training to seventy reps per set, and I was finally getting stronger. My technique and technical wrestling were becoming good, and the power I was getting started to help me execute moves in a more powerful and explosive way. That switch that had flipped in me—well, now it was a throttle, slowly increasing.

I started wrestling with more intensity and had a mission to make my opponent feel pain every time I grabbed them and did a move. The guys who made it to the top were tough and trained just as hard as I did. They meant business, and it was time for me to do the same. The aggression I started to unleash on my opponents may seem coarse or uncivilized, but I wasn't trying to permanently hurt someone. I just wanted them to think twice about testing me, which would help me dominate and impose my will on them.

There is no love in war. Rarely is there happiness during battle. And as a junior, I started internalizing the meanness and warlike nature I wrestled with. I wasn't this happy-go-lucky kid who was out there just to have fun and compete. I had a mission and knew I was going to beat someone up on the mat and enjoy the spoils after my victory. I was good at leg rides and certain other moves, and I knew if I got someone in it, I would punish my opponent badly instead of just scoring points. I enjoyed doing that, which helped me become more dominant in the sport. I would have to break my opponents mentally, through sheer force of will and punishment on the mat. Anyone who was at my level or higher would be trying to do the same to me, and it would come down to endurance.

This new mentality paid off. That year I took second in state at 145 pounds, and when we headed to junior nationals, I finally placed as a high schooler. More importantly I was programming myself to excel at a rapid rate. My mind and body were in sync like never before, and the guys that had beaten me in middle school or early high school years were no longer able to beat me. I was beating them on the mat every chance I got.

My senior year was when Bob came up with the infamous hundred-rep workouts. He came to the conclusion that one hundred reps each set was the sweet spot for muscle endurance, strength, and growth without causing injury. So that's what I did. One hundred reps of an arm exercise, then a hundred reps of a leg exercise, and back to a hundred reps of an upper body part, and right back to the lower body, until fifteen different exercises had been completed. It was an exhausting workout, but my body was able to handle it, and if a hundred reps of a certain exercise became too easy for me, then the weight would be increased. My body was going from lean, skinny, and wiry to having lean muscular mass and strength I hadn't had before. Between the weights and me growing, I went up in weight to wrestle at 154 pounds my senior year. I would walk around a little heavier, and those last two years of high school I would cut weight for my matches. That year, I started to plow through everyone. I wrestled tough and mean, and wanted my opponents on the ground, pinned.

I was able to pin forty-five guys that year, which was right around a national record, and I was the favorite going into the state tournament. But then, shit hit the fan. I got sick. Not just cold-and-cough sick, but fucking flu sick, no-energy type of sick. It felt like COVID before COVID even fuckin' existed. I never got sick, but for some reason this happened during the tournament. It felt like a nightmare. I didn't do well. That's where competing in a combat sport can work against you. Wrestling isn't similar to football, basketball, baseball, or any other team sport where if one player fucks up and feels shitty, then someone else can pick up the slack. When that whistle blows, it's a fuckin' hand-to-hand war, which means that winning falls on your shoulders, and unfortunately, so does losing.

After being undefeated, I lost twice in the tournament and ended up placing fifth. I don't show too much emotion when I win or lose, but I was pissed I didn't win state. But I was too sick to show it. The sickness had been my kryptonite, and I would never be a high school state champion.

After placing fifth, many of the potential scholarship offers faded, but California State University Fullerton (CSUF) decided to keep theirs on the table. I decided to sign with them even before the school year ended, but I still had unfinished business my senior year. After the disappointing ending to my high school season, I was back with Bob in San Clemente to prepare for my last junior nationals. Instead of the slow-paced folkstyle, I was once again training Greco-Roman and freestyle. I had a fire inside of me and wanted to prove my worth against the best in the country.

We headed to the University of Northern Iowa for the junior nationals, and I was focused. I entered in both Greco-Roman and freestyle tournaments and was demolishing my opponents.

Everything I had been taught, all the information that I had downloaded, I was putting into practice. I wrestled like Neo in *The Matrix*. I was able to see what my opponents were going to do and was going to impose my will and game plan on them. The only thing that could stop me was being sick. That had just been bad luck, though, and at the end of the junior nationals, I won both Greco-Roman and freestyle tournaments. I was able to technical fall (which is scoring fifteen points more than your opponent), pin nine out of ten opponents in Greco, and pin ten out of eleven in freestyle. Those kinds of stats were hard to come by. I finally was the best wrestler in my age and weight class in the entire country. I felt great. I had set a goal to win it, achieved that goal, and more importantly saw the hard work pay off.

My dad was ecstatic, and after placing first, scholarship offers started to pour in again. The only problem was I had already committed to CSUF, and I wasn't going to back out. I still had my sights set on Olympic gold, but I was a long way off from that. It was 1988 and I would now be competing with young men at the college level. Not to mention the men at the national level and world level competition were eons away from where I was. But I wasn't scared. I had to keep going. And for me, the only way to go was up.

★★★
3

OLYMPIAN AND THE DREAM TEAM

When I had been an underclassman, a lot of kids made prom night out to be some huge deal, a rite of passage of sorts, but when I was a senior, the allure wasn't the same. Still, I was able to have fun.

My dad had a small RV that he let me and five of my wrestling friends, along with our dates, take to the venue in Ontario, California. One of my Mormon friends, who didn't drink, was the designated driver while the rest of us were hitting a beer bong on the way down there. By the time we arrived, we had a pretty good buzz going.

I went dressed up like a chiseled-faced James Bond with a mullet. And wrestling wasn't the only thing I could do. I'm not going to win *Dancing with the Stars*, but I was able to dance. It helped that the top-forty pop music was far better in 1988 than today. George Michael, INXS, George Harrison, Guns N' Roses, Whitney Houston, Belinda Carlisle, Rick Astley, and Michael Jackson were just some of the artists blasting from the school's sub woofers.

After prom, we did a quick headcount and piled back into the mini RV. One of the girls must have not closed the door all the way, but as the RV crawled out of the parking lot, all I saw was the girl stumble against the door, and it swung open. Her momentum pulled her out of the door, and she grabbed onto the door handle for dear life. All I could see was her face and above the steps, her hand grabbing on, and her feet dangling on the pavement.

"Stop the car! Slow it down!" Someone beat me to telling our buddy to bring the RV to a halt, and when we stopped, the girl had a little bit of road rash on the top of her foot, but besides that, she was fine. All she needed was a band-aid and some rest. We double-checked the door to make sure it was closed and locked before we resumed our trip home.

When I got home, I tried to clean the stench of alcohol in the RV. I didn't want my dad to be too pissed from the smell. I couldn't seem to get the spilled-beer odor out, so I sprayed a shitload of cologne all over before going to bed. The next morning when I woke up, my dad asked me, "Dan, how come my RV smells like beer and cologne?"

After winning junior nationals and being on cloud nine, I knew I had *real* potential. My dad was happy, Bob was proud of me, and I had a newfound confidence in my abilities. The 1992 Olympics were four years away, but I already had thoughts of Olympic grandeur. I could see myself winning a gold medal. The problem was, there was no clear-cut plan for me to get there. I knew I needed more training, more wrestling, and better competition to improve.

When I got back to California following my victory, I didn't get a chance to dwell on it too long. After an uneventful high school graduation, I had three months of training and competing before moving to Fullerton for college. My first stop was Big Bear, California, a mountain city located in the Inland Empire of Southern California. Most people use mountain towns for skiing or lake vacations, but it was business as usual for me.

1988 was an Olympic year for Summer Games, and I was invited to a training camp where some of the American Olympic wrestlers were training. Besides the tourists and locals, many athletes, boxers, and fighters have used Big Bear, which is at an elevation of seven thousand feet, as a place to train before a season or a fight because of the lack of oxygen at that high altitude. It strengthens the lungs and gives athletes greater endurance to perform, which could potentially give them an edge over their opponent since most sports venues and stadiums are close to sea level. If you're not used to high elevation, it can seem like you're breathing out of a plastic bag.

"Dan, you see who's here?" My dad knew I recognized most of the guys as he was the one who'd brought me to watch them compete as a kid. One of the wrestlers I looked up to was Dave Schultz. He got to stand on the highest podium at the 1984 Olympics when he won a gold in freestyle wrestling. That's exactly where I wanted to be one day, hand over my heart as the red, white, and blue flag started its slow ascent atop the rafters. I couldn't wait for that day to make everyone proud.

In reality, I was a seventeen-year-old kid, a deer in headlights, wrestling with a fuckin' gold medalist, and a legend in the sport.

"You ready for a little wrestling?" Dave asked.

Was I ready? I pinched myself to make sure I wasn't daydreaming in English class. I heard a whistle blow, and there was Dave in front of me. Nope, I wasn't dreaming.

After we locked up together, I tried one of the moves that had worked on the best competition I faced previously. I tried to turn Dave and was shocked. That shit actually worked. It caught him off guard, but I was probably more surprised than him. Instead of countering me right away, he stopped. "Hey, that was a good move. How'd you do that?"

Dave could have easily mauled me, but oddly enough he wanted to learn from me. On what fuckin' planet does a wrestling GOAT (greatest of all time) ask a kid who's nuts just dropped down a few years before a wrestling question?

Dave taught me a valuable life lesson that day. *You can learn from anyone.* It didn't matter to him who the fuck he learned from. He just wanted to get better. Dave had no ego or pride, and, in my career, I took the same approach. Hear people out. Maybe they have some good shit to say. Maybe they don't. But you'll never know if you don't listen. You can't learn shit when you're talking.

I stayed in contact with Dave as I rose up the ranks, and even competed out of his wrestling club when the Jets folded. I watched more of his matches until his life came to an end in 1996. Dave was murdered by the financier of the wrestling club Foxcatcher, where he was coaching. It was sad to hear some wacko offed Dave for no fuckin' reason. Dave didn't even get a chance to pass on everything he knew to the next generation. He will still go down in American wrestling history as one of the best ever and has all the medals to back up his hall-of-fame career.

I was glad to see Hollywood take an interest in his life story several years ago and make a film with Mark Ruffalo playing Dave. Wrestling doesn't get a lot of shine, and even though it was under horrific circumstances, I'm glad Dave's legacy lives on.

Wrestling isn't for the faint of heart. Some kids do it only during the season, but for me, it was my life. It was a love-hate relationship. You love the sport but, at times, hate the day-in-and-day-out grind of it. When the hard work pays off, it's back to a love for it, for the natural art of hand-to-hand combat. That goes back even before the Greeks. In Genesis, Cain slayed Abel, and Samson was killing enemies with his hands. Even at seventeen, I had the wherewithal to take an untrained grown man out with my hands. I wanted to be able to conquer anybody.

I wrestled in two more tournaments before my freshman year officially started: the World Cup in Greece (in the seventeen-to-twenty-year-old division) where I didn't place, and the Olympic Trials in Boca Raton, Florida. I flat out got my ass kicked there. Those guys were the real deal, trained wrestling assassins who were at the peak of their careers, or close to it. I knew I wasn't ready for the big leagues yet, but it didn't deter me from my Olympic dreams. I *was* going to have to improve leaps and bounds in four years if I wanted that to happen.

I finally turned eighteen when I got to Cal State Fullerton. It was another pit stop for me, one that I thought would cover the next four to five years of my life. The university put me up in an apartment-style dorm across from the campus, which was pretty cool. And so were my three roommates. One was a wrestler on the team who was a couple years older than me, and the other two were regular students.

"Hey, Dan, you want to head to some parties?"

I'd go out with them to party a little bit, but I knew why I was there and never lost focus of the task at hand.

Right before the wrestling season started, I was asked by our head coach, Dan Lewis, if I wanted to sit out a year and redshirt. I told him I didn't know yet. I was still trying to figure out the best trajectory to get me to where I needed to be. A degree from a university seemed legit, but my mind was on Olympic gold.

Coach Lewis told me I needed to make a decision at the beginning of November. There was a senior on the team who was in the same weight division as me, which meant only one of us could compete for the university. He was in his last year of collegiate eligibility, so if I was to take the spot, that would end his college career.

To be fair, the Fullerton coaches put us head-to-head in a wrestle-off. The winner would get to compete while the loser would ride the pine. Equity in wrestling once again. No favoritism, no politics, just win, baby. Even though he was a few years older than me, I didn't feel out of my league. He was one of the better guys on the team, but when Coach Lewis blew the whistle for us to engage, I knew I could beat him. We wrestled one match, and I was able to defeat my senior counterpart. Coach Lewis didn't try to sway me one way or another. He said, "Good job, Dan. The spot is yours if you want it. Let me know by Monday."

I talked it over with my dad and Bob, to get their input. A redshirt year would give me more time to get stronger, and I'd still be able to wrestle competitively in Greco-Roman and freestyle tournaments. I opted to let the senior have one more year of glory, while I'd have a season to be out curfew free.

At the end of my freshman year, I rejoined the Jets and wrestled in both Greco and freestyle tournaments. I took second at the Espoir Nationals for the second year in a row. I was becoming more consistent at placing in the big tournaments.

In my second year, there would be no wrestle-offs. I would be the one competing in my weight division. The season started in November 1989, and I wasn't sure how I matched up against the best Division I wrestlers, but I found out right away when I lost my first few matches and thought, *Damn, how come my moves aren't working?* In high school, I was able to adapt to this style and beat guys handily. Division I wrestlers were levels above, and I had to go back to basics to find ways to beat them.

At the end of the season, my record was above .500, but not by much. I probably took fourth in the PAC-10 and flat out sucked. Hell, I didn't even make it to nationals. I thought I was better than how I performed, but the ruleset allowed the bigger, stronger dudes to stall their way to wins, which I underestimated.

After the shitty season, I still thought I'd go back to Fullerton. I had three years of eligibility left and had no plans of dropping out of college. I wasn't a ladies' man, but the shit was still fun. I could still fuck around at parties and have a good time. Plus, I couldn't visualize a pathway to the Olympics.

That all changed after I won the Espoir Nationals in Greco-Roman that summer. Bob told me the Jets had a sponsor who wanted to send five of us to train overseas, and I was one of the chosen ones if I accepted. The sponsor was Heath Sims's dad, who was able to get his company to fund us to train full-time with world-class competition and coaches. Heath was one of my teammates with the Jets, and his dad believed in our abilities and skills. (Heath was also one of the better wrestlers on the team, and he would make the 2000 Olympic team that went to Sydney.)

Bob told me if I took this opportunity to wrestle abroad, that meant I had to drop everything, including school. I would have to make wrestling my full-time job. I didn't care about chasing tail, I just wanted to be sure I was making the right decision. I knew who I could depend on to shoot it straight.

"You think it's a good idea, Dad? I will be out of the country for months at a time." Get an education, or roll the dice and be a college dropout. With a big decision like this, I wanted to see if my gut feeling was on. Dad was always logical and didn't make decisions based on emotion.

"Do you want to make the Olympic team?" he said.

It was 1990 and we were two years away from the 1992 games in Barcelona. How could I get good enough in time to beat every wrestler in my weight class in the United States? I started to get flashbacks of getting my ass handed to me in 1988. I knew there was no way I had the ability to make the team if the Olympics had been in 1990. My nuts were grown, but I was still learning how to drive a stick shift. I wasn't quite ready for the battlefront. And wrestling collegiate style wasn't going to do shit for me.

Bob needed an answer by the time school started. *Fuck. What am I going to do?* I needed to call Coach Lewis.

"Hello?"

"Hey, Coach, it's Dan."

"Hey, Dan, what's up? You going to be on campus next week?"

"That's what I was calling about, Coach. I've decided to drop out of school and wrestle Greco full-time."

"What? Dan, think about what you're saying."

"I know, Coach, but I gotta do it if I'm going to have a shot at making the Olympics."

"Dan, they're two years away. It's not enough time. I hate to say this, but I don't think you're going to make the team. Better to wait 'til you're done here."

"I gotta try, Coach."

"Dan, you're not fucking good enough to make that team. Okay? Don't make a dumb decision and throw away a scholarship. Get your education and degree. And, besides, who's going to compete for us in your weight class?"

"Thanks for everything, Coach. I've made my decision."

I hung up knowing I had to try. The belief I had in myself had never wavered. This was a golden opportunity. I couldn't let it go. I didn't have a family to care for, so I didn't need to finish my education like my dad had had to. I could travel, train, and focus on myself. My dad's selfless sacrifice when I was young helped put me in that position. All I had to do was work hard. Even though my dad was crazy, it was also probably genius. I could trek closer to my goals.

Instead of walking into the university halls of Cal State Fullerton, I had a light jacket on when I arrived in the Soviet Union in September 1990. Mikhail Gorbachev, who had been part of the Communist Party since 1985, had become head of state earlier that year. His communist beliefs had shifted more towards a social democracy system, so the country was turning in that direction. Basically, the country was all kinds of fucked up, but slowly changing.

Russians were constantly trying to trade us for anything we had. It didn't matter what it was. Everything we had was gold to them. They would offer us handmade souvenirs, these unique-looking dolls and big furry hats in exchange for our T-shirts, baseball hats, and shoes. There was a trade embargo then between the Soviet Union and United Sates, so it was impossible for anyone from the Soviet bloc to get their hands on anything from the States. If an American tourist happened to step foot over there, the Soviet government made it illegal to trade with us foreigners. That didn't stop them from trying, though.

When I was in Russia for the first time in 1987 as a high schooler, a teenage boy came up to us trying to trade. He must not have seen the cops glancing at us from around the corner. When he did, it was too late. The cops ran at him from different angles and tackled him. They beat the shit out of that kid then threw him in the back of a police car and hauled him off.

Gogi Parseghian, a Soviet immigrant, facilitated our training in the Soviet Union and other European countries. Gogi had come to America in hopes of competing for the United States in Greco-Roman wrestling and had won the 1988 and 1989 US Nationals. It was unfortunate because the US wouldn't let him compete since his official citizenship didn't kick in until after the 1988 Olympics.

Ironically, when he emigrated from the Soviet Union, he settled near San Clemente and the Jets training facility and had crossed paths with Bob. The rest was history. Bob was constantly looking for ways to improve our training and brought Gogi in to be one of our coaches. Bob was a true genius. Basically, teach your kids all the shit that you know. Those of us who had been with Bob and the Jets for a while needed to level up, and Gogi could help us get better by teaching us new techniques and connecting us with his former country, America's arch nemesis.

———————————————

I doubt there are a ton of people that would put Russia as their top spot for a travel destination, but I wasn't there for a tan or to go surfing. I was there to make an Olympic team. Most of the time we stayed at the Moscow Olympic Training Center, and several times we traveled to the Alushta Olympic Training Center (which is now in the Republic of Crimea). We also trained in the Russian cities of St. Petersburg, Rostov-on-Don, and Novosibirsk, and in Kiev (Ukraine), Minsk (Belarus), and Almaty (Kazakhstan).

Everywhere we went, the training was intense. Most of the coaches were former world or Olympic champs, and they *were* doing things a little bit better. In Greco-Roman wrestling, the margin of error is minute. The coaches were tweaking our technique and moves to make them tighter and smoother. This didn't mean that the Russians were physically or mentally tougher than Americans (there's always an exception, some American wrestlers were pussies, and there were some really tough Russians), but it was more the different nuances in matches that gave them an edge. They were taught and had drilled takedowns, throws, and other minor techniques that the Russian coaches had taught them, which made them better if all things were equal. Essentially, their wrestling history and technique made them superior to everyone else.

Those small tweaks were making me better, and I was taking in all the new information like a sponge absorbing water. My technique was becoming more refined with each session, and guys that had strength or brawn were easier for me to figure out and defeat. *Keep going, Dan.* I could *feel* myself getting better, but I knew to not be lax.

If I had been in school, the scholarship money would have taken care of my living expenses and meals at the university. Overseas, the sponsorship money was only able to cover lodging in the Olympic training center dorms and cafeteria food. The dorms were what you would expect from a communist country—basic, bleak, and barely bearable.

Our food consisted of three meals most days, with breakfast and dinner bringing what we called a "mystery meat" to the plate. Most of the time, I didn't know what the fuck they were serving us. On any given day it could've been horse, tongue, fish, or anything else that had a heart and moved around. Once in a while, we'd get eggs and potatoes with a layer of grease in the middle of the plate. Vegetables were hard to come by. It definitely wasn't a given. I don't know if it was because of their climate or lack of fertile land, but most of the time, there'd only be a protein and starch. I ate breakfast and dinner out of necessity. It was only at lunch where there would be a good-tasting meal. They would serve these hot, steaming soups that were great for recovery from our morning workout. But there were some days where I just couldn't get myself to eat some Russian Roulette food. I'd be like, *Fuck this food*, and head to the Russian McDonald's.

When training was done for the day, we would split off from the Russians to do our own workouts. One of the things I learned quickly was that wrestling was everything to those guys in the Soviet Union and Europe. I would watch them do a lot of calisthenics and certain exercises with kettle bells, then they'd go out and pummel or wrestle a little more around a track before running a couple of laps. Power cleaning was also a staple of their training, and it was interesting to see how much they could lift because they were good at it. Since they didn't have the same equipment we had back home, I would go out and do a hundred pull-ups, a hundred squats, a hundred bar dips, a hundred pushups (with a fifteen-second break in between), and then run up to three miles to finish the workout.

My new schedule consisted of heading to a tournament in Europe every couple of weeks with the Russians, then go back to Russia for training, compete in a tournament there, and travel home for a two-week break. It wasn't two weeks at the beach; we'd be training at the Jets facility, then go back to the Soviet Union to do it all over again. That was my life for the next year and a half. However, there would be exceptions.

At times our training took us to Sweden and Norway to train or compete in a tournament with the best there. The good thing about those countries was the food. They'd have fruit, granola, cheeses, sandwiches, meat, and fish. You didn't have to worry about eating a human corpse. But most of the time was spent in Russia and the Soviet bloc countries.

The cool thing was, I learned how to speak Russian and was able to make some extra money selling older-model shoes my buddy who owned a sporting goods store would give me. That gave me a little change to buy outside food when I didn't want to play spin the bottle with the cafeteria meals.

Living in a foreign land also made me more appreciative of growing up in the States. Every time we came back to America, I would be so thankful for the things I had. It seems that many Americans take liberty and freedom for granted. It didn't matter what Soviet bloc country I was in, or even Sweden or Norway, I just felt like America was the best country in the world, and seeing the things I did, it was clear that Americans just have it better.

In Russia, I would see people standing in lines for food or clothing on a regular basis, and everything was the same at the store. There was no variety. Only one type of glass, the same make and color of dishes, clothes looked alike, nothing was different. The people there had no individual expression. It felt glum, like people were merely going through the motions of life. That bleakness probably helped me improve quickly, because the lack of distractions allowed me to maintain my focus.

I started to see the fruits of my labor. I was always competing against the top five guys in every country I trained at or tournament I would compete in. And I would do well for the most part. At first, some of the guys threw me around a bit, but I learned to hang with anyone. There were certain moves I was able to get on my opponents and certain moves they could get on me, but I was always learning, trying to close the skill gap.

Craaaaaack. My neck just froze up. *Fuck. This shit is spasming. What the fuck?*

In October 1991, I was back in Russia wrestling in a tournament when this big, strong guy I was competing against held my head down for most of the match. *Another one of these fuckers.* He knew he didn't have the skill to beat me with technique, so he was trying to use his brute strength to get me to fold. I didn't. I ended up beating him, but my neck immediately froze up on me after the match. *I can get through this, no big deal. Suck it up.*

The 1992 US Olympic Trials were less than a year away, and I couldn't let all this training go to waste. I didn't know how bad the injury was, so I decided to just train through it. Besides, our sponsorship money had dried up, and we had about two months of training left until returning home for good. But before we could travel back, the shit hit the fan in December.

"Dad, we're stuck." My dad was confused when I called him from Moscow to let him know we needed help.

"What are you talking about, Dan?"

"They're not giving us visas to fly home."

"What? Why?"

"The Russian coaches said they haven't received payment for our training and expenses the past few months. They said we're not going home until they get paid."

Damn. Are we being kept hostage? I had never dealt with the money or transfer of it. All I knew was that the coaches were pissed. My Russian was good enough to know that we weren't going anywhere without payment. Basically, we were fucked. We had no money to pay them, and without a travel visa, we might as well kiss freedom goodbye. There would be no friendly exchange of citizens here. We needed help.

It was Gogi who came up with a plan. Even though he was now an American citizen, he still had friends in Russia. One of Gogi's buddies worked at the airport and said he could get the five of us travel visas for $100 each. There was only one caveat. Once the visas were issued, there was a good chance the coaches would be alerted about them, so once we got them, we had to figure out a way to sneak out or be ready for a long, brutal winter.

Knock, knock. I opened my dorm room door to Gogi.

"Dan, we gotta go. Go get the other guys."

"What happened?" I said.

"All the coaches left for South Africa for a tournament. But it's a quick turnaround. They'll be back in a day or so. We gotta leave now."

We packed our shit and headed straight to the airport. It was a few days before Christmas, so there were more people out than usual. I was like Matt Damon in the Jason Bourne movies, looking around to see if anyone recognized us as we headed out. And none of us had cash. I had a $500 limit credit card, which barely covered our visas, and my dad had to cover some of the flights. *This is going to be interesting.* I was calm and cool, but I was still aware of my surroundings. After going through Russian Customs, I was waiting for one of our coaches to yell in Russian, "Hey, where you all going?" but it didn't happen. We boarded our flight, and it wasn't until we took off that I knew we'd made it out. When the coaches found out we were back in America, they were mad as fuck. But there was nothing they could do. It wasn't like we didn't want to pay them. But Russians are pretty smart. This wouldn't be the last I heard from them.

In January 1992, a few weeks after being home, I wanted to know how fucked up my neck was and headed to the doctor. The pain hadn't gone away. I had simply learned how to adapt by tilting my head forward to take some of the pressure away. If I didn't, I would feel more fucked up. With my head looking straight, three fingers on my left hand would go numb. I would have to put my head straight down, chin to chest, to not lose any feeling.

My doctor referred me to a neurosurgeon, and when they did an MRI, he found three herniated disks in my C4, C5, C6, and C7. Surgery was an option, but if I went that route, that would put me out of any hope for Olympic gold that year. The neurosurgeon knew what was at stake, and after further examination, said I would be able to continue competing if I could withstand the pain. The tissues in my neck had calcified just enough to stabilize it. Plus, I have a big neck. The average man's neck is about 15 inches in circumference, with 17 inches being on the larger side. My neck is a girthy 18.5 inches. The years of rigorous wrestling and weight training had put a decent amount of muscle in my neck.

Well, here we go. Let's see how good you've gotten, Dan. In March of 1992, I had my first test to see how my skills compared against my fellow countrymen. I wasn't a seventeen-year-old boy anymore whose balls had just started to hang. I was like an anime character who had trained in some far away land and had gotten a hundred times better.

At the Olympic qualifier, I wasn't ready to cut a lot of weight yet, so I competed at 198 pounds, which was 18 pounds outside my natural weight class of 180. I knew if I lost, I would still have a chance to get to the Olympic Trials. I didn't lose—I won that tournament, which qualified me, and then headed to Las Vegas in April for nationals. I wrestled again at 198 pounds, but that time I took fourth. *Damn. Those guys were still kind of big for me.*

"So, you decide what weight you're going to do, Dan," Bob asked.

My dad and Bob already knew I was thinking of cutting weight to get down to 180 for the Olympic Trials, and it made sense since those guys were my size. I knew what I was going to do.

"I'll get down to 180."

I headed to Albany in June for the trials, which was a wrestle-off with four guys that were ranked fourth place through eighth place. *Okay, Dan, you can do this. Lose one match, and go home. Fuck that.* I beat every guy on day one, then had ninety minutes to make weight after my last match, to wrestle the third-ranked guy the next day. I made weight and mentally prepared myself for the format change in the final matches. It would now be a best-out-of-three series. If I lost one match, I could still move on.

On day two, I was familiar with my first opponent. He was ranked third in the nation and was older with much more experience than me. It definitely showed in the first match. He beat me 7–0. *It's okay, Dan. You've got him figured out now.* I knew if I lost the next match, it would be over for me. But I wasn't nervous. I won the second match by a couple points, and in the third match, I demolished him. I got a little break, then had to go against the number-two guy.

I beat him and then the number-one-ranked guy that same day, which still didn't put me in the Olympics. I had to beat the previous year's top guy. I had ninety minutes that day to make weight one more time—or forfeit. I had put on ten to twelve pounds in a day, and my body was exhausted from the gauntlet of matches, and I barely made weight that final time.

I had four days off before the final match. If I won, I'd finally become an Olympian. Lose, and it'd be four years of what the fuck. I didn't want to be runner-up, but I could tell I was so much better. I wouldn't have beaten any of those guys the year before.

The finals were set for another best-out-of-three format. I didn't know what to expect, but I beat him in two matches and said, "Fuck yeah," on the inside. Somehow that had become my victory chant, and I would continue to say that after every big match or big knockout when I got into mixed martial arts.

After my win, the Russian coaches caught wind of my victory, and instead of sending congratulations, they sought their outstanding payment. They figured if they went to the International Wrestling Committee, they might be able to find a way to recoup the $25,000 unpaid bill. They were trying to sanction me for the money, even though there were five of us. But I was the only one from that group to make the Olympic team, so it made sense. I wasn't sure if the IWC was going to see the sanctions through, but I told them it wouldn't be necessary. I would raise the money to pay them. I put on fundraisers to help pay the entire bill, which I was able to get the Russian coaches right before the Olympics started.

"Please fill this form out and please be as detailed as possible."

I was in Colorado Springs, home to the US Olympic headquarters, and the medical staff needed to clear me for competition. They wanted me to list any injuries I had before they conducted a physical. Even though I knew my neck was fucked up, I was hesitant about putting it on the stupid form because those are the type of people that will look for anything to keep you from competing. They wanted to know if you had a damn paper cut.

I didn't want to be disqualified for some dumb shit like lying, so I ended up writing that I had a minor neck injury. I sure as hell wasn't going to say that I had two herniated disks.

After I turned in my paperwork, the medical staff looked it over and said, "Wow, a neck injury? We're going to have to take you to get an MRI."

What the fuck? This can't be happening. These motherfuckers don't want me to wrestle. Didn't they know I had just competed in ten matches?

"Fuck you," I said to no one in particular. "I'm going to the Olympics."

The staff looked stunned. "What?" one of them said.

"I am wrestling in the Olympics. My neurosurgeon already signed off on this injury. I was already cleared."

I was pissed. There was no way they were going to take my dreams away from me. But it was out of my hands. After consulting with each other, one of the staff members said they'd have to take me in to get an MRI and get one of their doctors to clear me. I didn't have a choice, so I agreed and we headed off to the doctor.

The staff member I rode with was cool and understood where I was coming from. She was surprised I was able to even walk with my neck injury and said most athletes probably wouldn't have competed without surgery, or they would've been flat-out denied. But there was no way they could take this from me. Taking a ride to see the doctor seemed like a waste of time to me.

When we got there, I made sure to be calm. A smile can go a long way. The doctor gave me an MRI, and I explained to him the situation about my neck. He could see how bad I wanted to compete. He called my neurosurgeon in California, and after doing some tests, he agreed. "Okay, Dan, yep, you're good to go. Here ya go." The doctor signed my medicals and cleared me to compete. *Whew*. That was close.

Tock, tock, tock. I looked down at my feet when I boarded the Olympic plane. I couldn't believe it. We left the US about ten days before the Olympics started. It felt like I was going to war with my fellow Olympians. We had the same mission with different skillsets.

While I was on the massive chartered Boeing 747, it started to hit me a little bit more. This kid from the small dusty town of Victorville, California, had beat out everyone in the country. But I knew my work wasn't done. I wasn't satisfied to be the best in the US, I wanted to be the best in the world. I was still the happiest twenty-one-year-old on the planet and even prouder to represent the United States. When most twenty-one-year-olds were probably enjoying the nightlife for the first time, I was reflecting on what I needed to win gold as we were flying over the Atlantic Ocean. *Coach Lewis was wrong.*

We landed in the medieval city of Carcassonne, France, where we would train and acclimate to the time difference before heading to Barcelona. The city was badass because it was old and seemed like it had a lot of cool history. Carcassonne's roots went back to 3500 BC, and they have a ginormous castle, the Cité de Carcassonne, which was built back in the Gallo-Roman era. One glance at it and you're like *holy shit*. It's got two layers of fortified walls and a huge drawbridge. The only thing missing was a princess.

It was cool to see and wonder what some of the battles might have looked like back then. Knights in some fuckin' shining armor shooting arrows at each other and fighting with swords to the death. If I lived back then instead of drilling takedowns, I probably would've been trying to drill a hole in someone's chest with my medieval weapon of choice. But I wasn't there for blood, I was just there to impose my will on my opponents mano a mano.

"Hey, Dan, how you feeling?"

I turned and saw a guy I had just met two months prior, fellow American wrestler Randy Couture.

"What's up, Randy, I'm feeling good. I'm ready to go."

I'd met Randy and warmed up with him at the Olympic Trials in California. He was there competing at 198 pounds, and I had asked him if he could warm up with me before one of my matches. Randy had won nationals the year before, and if that had been an Olympic year, he would've been the one to compete in the Olympics, but he lost in the finals of the '92 trials.

Randy had been in the Army for a few years and worked his way up to sergeant. He's always been a patriot and team player, and we had a lot in common. At that time nobody knew what we would accomplish in our careers. Randy would become a five-time UFC champion in two weight divisions and one of the greatest fighters ever. But in 1992, the UFC and mixed martial arts weren't around, so to pay bills and keep his Olympic dream alive at twenty-nine, Randy worked as an assistant wrestling coach at Oregon State. There were no thoughts of him acting in blockbuster films (*The Expendables* trilogy) or starring alongside Sylvester Stallone, Jason Statham, Mickey Rourke, Jet Li, and Michael Jai White. He was just Randy, a Greco-Roman buddy who was becoming my friend, and someone that wanted Olympic gold one day as well. That trip in Carcassonne and Barcelona was the beginning of our long friendship.

Fweeeeeet!

"Stop! Dan you might want to take a look in the mirror at your teeth."

I was wrestling with one of my Olympic teammates when an accidental knee to my face stopped the action. There were only a few days left before we headed to Barcelona, and the only thing I could think was, *Why do I need to look at my teeth?* I was defending a move while my partner was hopping in, and as I turned towards him, I took a knee to my teeth. I felt fine, but as I ran a finger across my teeth, I thought *Damn. They are out of place a little bit.* When I looked in the mirror, I saw that my front teeth were bent forty-five degrees, so I thought maybe I could fix them myself. I pushed them back, and they snapped in place, but the teeth were still loose. It felt like the bone around the teeth was broken, but not the teeth themselves. Randy came along as I headed to a local dentist where they wired them in place. I wasn't happy about having to take the time to get my shit wired, but I wasn't going to whine about it either—I still had more training to do.

We left Carcassonne two days before the Opening Ceremonies and finally made it to Spain. Barcelona's Olympic Village (the designated place where all the athletes stay) had brand-new condos for our living quarters. The developers of the condos were smart. They had planned the building of the complex to align with the Olympics, so right after housing the Olympians, they could sell the units.

It was kind of cool to take everything in at the Olympic Village. I was able to see the dynamics of the other athletes and different people from different cultures all across the world. And there was a mixture of athletes that had competed before along with many first-timers like me. You could see athletes from just about every country eyeing each other. It was like a smorgasbord of pure testosterone and estrogen. There was *definitely* some sexual tension too. To my surprise, I saw a decent amount of fucking going on. (After I was done competing, I may or may not have gotten friendly with one or two athletes.) But, for the most part, what happened at Olympic Village stayed at the Village.

The day of Opening Ceremonies was a surreal, out-of-body experience. I had really made it. It wasn't a dream or a joke. Barring some freak accident, I would actually compete and try to win gold. The first part of my dreams had come true.

I waited with my fellow Americans and other Olympians inside of an arena next to the stadium we were set to walk out to. The countries are introduced in alphabetical order, so we were about middle of the pack since United States is spelled Estados Unidos in Spanish.

The 1992 Games was the first year that professional basketball players from the NBA could compete at the Olympics. The media made a big hoopla over it, which boosted viewership. It was fuckin' cool to think I was in the same Olympic Games as Michael Jordan, Magic Johnson, and Larry Bird, but I never thought I'd see any of those guys. Besides, we'd been told if we saw them not to ask for a picture. In fact, the US Olympic Committee told us to not bring a camera with us period. But it seemed like every American Olympian had a camera with them.

When they finally called "Estados Unidos" to walk out, I kind of lost my place. Maybe I was taking in everything too well. I was told to hurry up since I was close to the back. While I made my way toward the stadium tunnel entrance, I saw some genuine giants come from the side to join in. *Oh shit, it's the Dream Team*, I thought. There, walking with me, were the biggest names in basketball— Magic Johnson, Larry Bird, Michael Jordan, Scottie Pippen, Charles Barkley, Patrick Ewing, David Robinson, John Stockton, Karl Malone, Clyde Drexler, Chris Mullin, and Christian Laettner. I looked right next to me, and there was a familiar face from television, Scottie Pippen, walking alongside me. I'm 5'11", but I felt much shorter next to him and the others.

When we reached our spot, I stood back as athletes ran up to ask for pictures. Everybody seemed happy to be there, and the NBA guys could have cared less about the no-picture rule, but when I looked next to me, Scottie Pippen looked annoyed. Most of the athletes were asking for pictures with Magic or Jordan. Maybe he was mad that no one was running up to him, but every time I glanced over at him, I saw him rolling his eyes at the attention the other guys were getting, especially Magic.

Suddenly, all the stadium lights went out, and everyone's attention shifted to the Olympic torch. I got fuckin' goosebumps being present for the action. There was no announcement of what the fuck was going to happen, but I saw the dude with the torch bring it close to Spanish archer Antonio Rebollo's bow and *plume!* The arrow flared up as radiant orange flames engulfed the tip. Antonio took aim up high, drew his bow, and shot the flaming arrow out of the stadium and right into a giant cauldron filled with gas and propane that set the whole thing ablaze. It was fuckin' awesome. I went from having goosebumps to my hair sticking up on the back of my neck.

My first match was a couple days later. By then, the Opening Ceremonies adrenaline had faded, but I felt good.

I was pitted against Egyptian Mohyeldin Ramadan in the opening round, and as soon as the match started, I thought, *What the fuck is he doing?* I had a mullet and could feel Ramadan pulling my hair. No one had ever grabbed my hair in a match. That is some pussy shit, and the ref didn't say a word. It wasn't affecting me too much, but the motherfucker kept doing it. Then, when the ref put me on the ground, Ramadan would maneuver a gut wrench and grab my nuts with one hand to try and use my balls to turn me. He was wrestling *dirty as fuck.* If he thought that would soften me up, he was wrong. I got meaner during the match and proceeded to beat the fuck out of him, winning 4–0. *War was in session.*

I didn't want to get my hair pulled in my next match, so I put my mullet in a ponytail when I took on Frenchman Martial Mischler. Beating him 7–2 gave me more confidence. I thought I had real shot to win this thing, even though these guys seemed to be playing under a different set of rules. But in the third match, the fuckery started again. I lost 2–0 and couldn't believe it. The match was close, but I thought I had done enough to win and was surprised how the ref and judges scored it. I kept my mouth shut, didn't complain, but it felt like I was in some forbidden, unwelcome place.

Match four was against the current Greco-Roman world champion, Péter Farkas. This seemed like a gold-medal match. The winner would probably be on top of the winner's podium. I knew Farkas was good, but I thought I was better. The ref faced us off and we shook hands. As soon as we clinched and I felt his skin, I backed off. *Why are my hands oily?* I looked to the ref and tried to call timeout, but he gestured to keep wrestling. *This fucker is greased up.* I was pissed that my hand was slimy and slippery. Was I in the Olympics or some Mickey Mouse tournament? No one had ever tried this shit on me before, but I stayed calm.

We clinched like two rams whose horns are locked together, and at one point in the match, the referee called him for passivity. That meant I was able to get top position, which was one of my specialty positions. I clasped my hands around him, and it felt like I would be able to get enough leverage to start a good lift. *Just finish the move, Dan.* The lift worked. I had Farkas halfway up in the air about to throw the cheating fuck and score a minimum of four points, but something started to go wrong. I felt my hands slipping apart. He must have had layers of oil on his body. My grip broke and I lost the hold. That had never happened before. It was like a bad dream, but the shit was real. I had never experienced the cheating bullshit before, and I ended up losing 2–0 to the Hungarian. Had I landed that one move, it would have won me the match and put me in the top four.

There was no point in complaining after the match. I knew they didn't care. I couldn't wrap my head around the lack of sportsmanship. The dream kept getting worse.

I lost my next match 6–0, and for my final match, which determined ninth place, I got fucked once again. I wrestled against Switzerland's David Martinetti, who I was scoring on with ease. Or so I thought. When I looked at the score, I was stunned to see that I was losing. I figured I'd at least placed in the top nine, but that wasn't going to happen. Instead of my hand being raised, they announced Martinetti the winner. It was a bullshit win for him, and the real-life nightmare was finally over. One of the commentators, Jeff Blatnick, came up to me and told me he scored the match in my favor.

I didn't know who he was but was still trying to wrap my head around his victory. It turned out Martinetti was related to Raphaël Martinetti, the head of the International Federation of Associated Wrestling Styles (FILA) officiating committee. No conflict of interest there, right? A relative in charge of the officials, no big deal, huh?

Raphaël would become president of FILA ten years later and in 2020 was ordered by the Swiss government to pay taxes on millions of dollars he and his wife accepted as "donations" by individuals from Azerbaijan. Go fuckin' figure.

I might sound bitter, but I wasn't. I had lost before, but I knew when someone was better than me. It was the lack of sportsmanship at what was supposed to be the highest level of competition that really got to me. I left Barcelona with a sour taste in my mouth. I was the tenth best wrestler in the entire world at 180 pounds, but had I not gotten screwed over, would I have come out on top? I'll never know, but it felt like being in grade school on the baseball team all over again. Who would have thought there would be politics at the Olympics? To top it off, Farkas and his greased-up body went on to win gold.

☆☆☆
4

THE TERMINATOR, GOLD AGAIN, AND CHELSEA CLINTON

Soon after we had gotten back to the States from Barcelona, the majority of the Olympians took a charter flight to Washington, DC, where these giant buses picked us up from the airport and caravanned us to the White House. I felt like I was in a James Bond movie. When we pulled up to the White House gates, we had to show the Secret Service our Olympic badges as we got off the bus and made our way through the metal detectors.

We were told that President George Bush Sr. had planned a picnic for us on the White House lawn, and as we pulled up, I saw these fancy picnic tables arranged in perfect symmetry with place settings that made it look like a five-star restaurant. I guess someone forgot to check the forecast that day because rain started pouring down. There was no way they were going to let us get soaked, so word came down for all of us to go inside.

You ever go to sleep as a kid thinking about your dreams and goals for your future, then wake up and it becomes a reality? I couldn't believe I was in America's most famous residence. I closed my eyes for a few seconds to make sure I wasn't dreaming. At first, it felt surreal, like an out-of-body experience, but then, it felt real as hell when I found myself standing next to The Terminator, Arnold Schwarzenegger, and shaking his hand. *He's a lot smaller in person*, I thought.

I didn't know what to expect from him. I had no idea he would even be at the White House. He was the biggest blockbuster action star at the time, and I half expected him to go into Terminator Mode. I was surprised that Arnold was only an inch taller than me, but he had these massive python arms. After shaking his hand, all I was thinking of when I turned back to him was, "I'll be bock," but the former Mr. Olympia was cool. There was no need to turn The Terminator into a pretzel.

I felt like a nobody; I wasn't anything special; I hadn't medaled, yet they still invited a mullet-cut, college dropout into a historic building. I would have traded in a White House visit with gold, but I was still grateful to be there.

The rain outside didn't derail the president from honoring our hard work. In war, sometimes you have to improvise. If you're down in wrestling, sometimes the only way to win is to go for broke, while other times being strategic will win you a match. The White House staff improvised. There was no time to prep for five hundred people coming indoors, so we were directed to sit on the high-gloss floors, windowsill ledges, or in elaborate-looking side rooms that could have been out of a Harry Potter book. The chefs had made burgers, hot dogs, potato salad, and chips for our rained-out picnic lunch. When I looked around, I couldn't believe how big the interior was, and all the historic, cool shit strategically placed around. When I got my food, I didn't think burgers or hot dogs could taste that good. It was one of the most memorable meals I've ever had.

"Hello, how's it going?"

I guess I had been daydreaming again, trying to take everything in. When I looked to see who was talking to me, there he was, President Bush. He offered his hand, and I quickly grabbed my napkin to get the salt and shit off of it.

"Nice to meet you, Mister President," I said.

"Everything going okay?" he asked.

"Yes it is, thank you."

I hadn't even medaled, and he still shook my hand. I watched President Bush make his way around the room, shaking hands with all of the athletes. I thought that was pretty badass that the president of the United States respected us enough to make his way around and be personable with everyone.

I was trying to figure out what to do following the Olympics. Should I go left, right, or straight ahead? I may not have been the smartest twenty-one-year-old, but I was definitely one of the most resilient. My mind was on wanting to go back in four years, I just didn't know what my immediate future held.

When I was in Barcelona, some of the coaches from various universities found out I had one year left of NCAA eligibility and tried to recruit me. USA freestyle wrestling coach Lee Roy Smith was stepping down from coaching the national team to become the new head coach at Arizona State University. He offered me a scholarship, as did Michigan State University and a few other colleges.

I hadn't thought out my next move but have always been one to take opportunities when they arise. Go with the flow. Or, like Bruce Lee said, "Be like water."

Eventually, I decided to attend ASU; it felt like it was the right move. Arizona was only a drive away from California, and I've never been too fond of cold weather. In Michigan, my balls probably would've froze. I didn't have to worry about that in the Arizona desert.

It was a little weird going back to school just a few weeks after the Olympics and meeting the president. I had just turned twenty-two; the last time I had been on a college campus, I had been just shy of twenty, yet there I was, once again, with a backpack on, books in one hand and a few pencils in the other. It's funny how life works sometimes. One day you're at some immaculate-looking medieval castle, the next day you're in a university lecture room. I never thought my accomplishments made me better or worse than anyone, so I didn't mind the change. I did like the social aspect of school, and a few people on campus recognized me from the Olympics. Even though ASU was a fun school known for good parties, I still had gold on my mind.

The shitty thing was that I was going to have to start the process all over again. The Olympics would be in Atlanta, and I knew everyone in my weight class was vying to take the top spot to represent the US. Wrestling teaches you patience. No one is good right away, so at least I knew how to navigate the next four years. In war, only fools rush in with no game plan. It's a suicide mission if you proceed with no patience.

When the season started, I was back to the collegiate style of wrestling. It took some time to adjust to the rules again. Coach Smith wanted me to wrestle at 190 pounds, but I told him I thought I'd be too small for some of the guys, especially with that style. Going down a weight class would have served me much better. He overruled me, but I was right. I won the PAC-10 and made it to nationals, but lost to the bigger, stronger dudes in the nation.

After the season, my college eligibility ended. I thought I might be granted an extra year of my academic scholarship because I had only been able to compete for two years between Fullerton and ASU, but the university refused. The NCAA started my eligibility "clock" following my redshirt freshman year. No more beer pong parties. The NCAA has since changed the rules, allowing student athletes an extra year of eligibility if they compete at the Olympics.

The next year, in April 1993, I won the Greco-Roman Nationals, then doubled up as the winner of the World Team Trials in June. I had to win every year to be the number-one guy in the United States at 180 pounds. A loss would take away that status and the measly money that came along with it. That fall, I was slated to compete in the World Tournament. My neck was still fucked, but now I could feel something with my shoulder. If I had to compete, I could've blocked out the pain, but I wanted to get the shit fixed if something was wrong. For all I knew it might not have been serious.

It was July 1993 when I found myself on the cutting table. I dropped out of college since my scholarship only covered me when I competed for ASU, so paying for school was out of the question, and I decided to go under the knife and get my shoulder fixed.

The doctor said it looked pretty bad. The bicep tendon was torn and detached from my shoulder, and my rotator cuff and labrum were fucked too. It had been screwed up for the past three years, but I never thought much of it. It happened in the university nationals in 1990; I lifted someone in a weird way, and he landed on my shoulder, which made it pop. It hadn't felt good, but I still finished the tournament. And it wasn't painful all the time. I told myself it was just a little tightness, nothing to worry about.

The doctor was more shocked than me that I had wrestled with it torn for so long. He scratched his head and tried to reason how I was able to wrestle in nationals, college, and the Olympics. I think he thought I was a freak show and hypothesized that since my muscles were so dense, that must have helped keep my shoulder in place, just like my neck.

I don't especially care for doctors putting me to sleep, because I'd rather just feel the pain and get through it. For that surgery, I had no choice. They had to knock me out so they could lift my arm over my head, and it popped out of the socket on its own because it was all fucked up. They had to put in overtime to repair and connect the tissue. I didn't feel anything. They knocked me out with enough tranquilizer to put a horse down.

The surgery was mostly a success, although I can still feel my arm shift around in the socket. At least the arm is still there. Hell, if my dad was my doctor, he probably would've told me to put some ice and a big-ass band-aid on it.

Alright, Dan, go easy. Just let your arm heal.

When I got back to California, I moved with some roommates to Huntington Beach, not far from the Jets facility in San Clemente and only a couple hours from my parents. USA Wrestling had paid for my surgery, but I was going to lose the top spot on the National Team, since I wasn't going to be able to train or compete for them. That was just the rules. The show must go on, a new piece of meat coming in.

If that wasn't enough, I was broke as fuck. After the Olympics, I was getting a $650-a-month stipend for being the number-one guy, but I had no sponsorships or endorsement deals. Not even one of those local used-car dealerships reached out to me to do a commercial. Wrestling wasn't looked at as a cool sport back then like basketball, swimming, or gymnastics. It's just coming around now, and Olympic wrestlers were on their own. It definitely wasn't a way to make a living. But that didn't deter me. I wasn't wrestling for money or for anyone else. I wrestled because I loved it. Even with the fucked-up neck, mangled shoulder, and mutant muscles I had. I was determined to be the best in the world.

"Grab the weight with your hand, then slowly bring it up to you."

Fuck, it feels like I'm in kindergarten, I muttered to myself. Rehab or training? If you're in rehab, then your ass isn't training, and that's all I wanted to do. But there I was, watching paint dry, my physical therapist treating my shoulder like it was a baby's.

"Does that hurt?" my physical therapist asked.

"No, it's fine. Can we add one more weight?"

It took me a few weeks of rehab going three days a week to get the green light from my doctor to get back in the gym and train lightly. But I was drilling even without the doctor's approval. Besides, my shoulder improved quickly, and in January 1994, I was already training with the National Team in Colorado Springs.

After I got my shoulder checked out a gazillion times, the doctors said it would never fully heal, but I didn't care. I could compete with my shoulder at 70 percent. In April, I placed first at nationals, and a few months later, after I took first at the World Team Trials in June, I was back to making the top money, $650 a month.

Things changed in 1995. The World Team Trials were in Atlanta, and USA Wrestling probably thought it would be smart to have the Trials there to get a feel for the 1996 Olympics. In the finals, I lost and was dropped from the top guy to number two for the rest of that year. Even though I had a shitty finals, I was glad when Randy and Heath won their weight classes. We could never seem to be the number-one guys the same year.

That night, to celebrate their wins, we went out for a few drinks in Buckhead, a town right outside of Atlanta, and as we were bar hopping, Randy bumped into a parked car. The next thing we knew, this bouncer dude came out with a big stick talking shit to Randy.

"What the fuck, you guys come back for more?" he said.

I didn't know what the fuck he meant. Randy quickly responded, "Dude, what are you talking about?"

The bouncer kept coming forward, a posse of fellow bouncers behind him. I thought, *Shit, the OK Corral all over again.* Randy wasn't going to let the bouncer hit him with the big-ass stick, so he grabbed it with one hand and the dude's throat with the other. The fight was on. Two bouncers came at me, and another one went at one of the wrestlers with us, as a couple of chicks with us started to freak out.

Whewwf. I shoved the shit out of the first bouncer who tried to grab me, then went from prey to predator. I grabbed the second bouncer and pushed him down while holding his legs after his ass tried to crawl away. "Oh, you want some too, fucker? Shouldn't have tried to grab me." I started talking shit to him as I had him pinned down and punched him a few times but looked to see if Idiot #1 had gotten up from his tumble. At some point during the drunken Royal Rumble, my shirt got pushed way over my head. I could hear people yelling for us to stop, so I momentarily paused my beatdown over Idiot #2 because I couldn't see shit with my shirt over my face. I don't know if it was friend or foe, but someone grabbed my shirt and threw it. I looked around to get my bearings and saw Randy had one of the bouncers in a headlock and was fucking him up. The bouncers had bitten off a little more than they could chew. They clearly hadn't expected us to be that tough.

"Dan, get the fuck out of here, the cops are coming," a sober-sounding voice yelled out.

I could see the bouncers were ready to call it quits. We weren't the instigators or bullies, so when they started wiping themselves off and backing up, we were good to be done as well. Someone threw me my shirt, which had been flung into the darkness, and I put it on like nothing happened, and we walked off.

The next day, we found out the bouncers mistook us for a group of guys who'd tried to fuck with them. Either that, or those guys pissed them off to the point that they tried to take it out on us. That same day, Randy had an outing with USA Wrestling's board of directors, where he was an athlete's rep. Coincidentally, the meeting was at the exact same place where the mayhem had gone down the day before. Randy didn't recognize the place or the bouncers, but they recognized him. They called the cops, and he was escorted out.

When I headed into the 1996 Olympic Trials, I was the number-two guy in the nation. I felt good and confident that I had improved, but ten days before the trials, I suffered another minor setback. While I was training with Heath and pushing down on his head, he popped his head up right into my mouth. My mouth felt a little funny, and I bit down on my mouthpiece not knowing what to expect. *Crunch.* My front tooth was loose, and I could feel it wiggling around. I thought it might be okay, but it was broken. *Fuck.* What do we need teeth for anyways? Food can be blended.

I headed to the dentist, and he gave me a removable retainer with a tooth on it called a "flipper." It felt weird at first, but what's one missing tooth? I ended up losing three more in my career. The next one to a frisbee football game, another sparring with Randy, and the last one in a fight with "Big Nog," Antônio "Minotauro" Nogueira.

I headed north for the Greco-Roman Olympic Trials and was surprised by the choice of venue. You would think USA Wrestling would have held the final tournament at a university or in a nice facility, but we were given a rinky-dink high school gym in San Jose, about an hour away from San Francisco. I had been to better middle school gyms than this one, but there I was with Randy and Heath, all of us looking to make the Olympic team. When we walked into the gym, we couldn't believe it.

"This shit sucks," I told Randy.

"It's got to be at least a hundred and five in here," he said.

The gym lights were already hot, but ESPN made it worse. They were covering the event and had these bright-ass heat lamps lighting up the whole gym. There was no air conditioning to mitigate the heat, *and* all the fans were broken. It felt like a fuckin' sauna. The California summer heat had nothing on the oven inside the gym.

When I found out the Freestyle Olympic Trials were held in a nice, air-conditioned arena in Seattle, I was thinking, *What the fuck?* But that's how USA Wrestling treated Greco-Roman guys. Freestyle is more popular in America, whereas overseas, Greco is the top style. Greco is so popular in Europe, some countries don't even have freestyle teams.

I weighed in the first day and was ready to get to work. In the worst conditions I've ever wrestled in, I won all my matches, then weighed in again for the finals match. Once again, four years of work was coming down to one last opponent. If I lost, that was it.

The finals were best-out-of-three, and I knew my opponent was tough. I had beaten his brother to make the 1992 Olympic team, so this guy wasn't going to be no pushover. On top of that, the gym heat had sucked out some of my energy the day before. My opponent was bigger and stronger than me, and he preferred sloppy matches. The extreme heat meant more sweat on the mat, which was an advantage for him.

After the first two matches, it was 1–1. Going into that third match, there was nothing I hadn't seen. I was almost twenty-six and had competed at the highest levels for the past four years. I just had to find a way to win one more match. And I didn't have to worry about getting cheated by judges or referees. There were no politics amongst the USA Wrestling refs. They weren't biased like the Olympic refs. They wanted the best guys representing America.

The last match went back and forth. He knew what my game was, and we were able to counter each other well. No one wanted to lose. You talk about a lonely trip back home. Most professional athletes who lose a championship have an opportunity to be there the next year. In boxing or fighting, a rematch can happen within months. But four years being shaved off your life before getting that same opportunity—it can drive someone mad, and many don't ever get that opportunity again.

The whistle blew. Time was up. I looked at the scoreboard, and we were headed to sudden death. I had to score in overtime or else I'd lose. *C'mon, Dan, just a little bit longer.*

"Alright, guys, first one to score wins," the ref said.

Fweeet! We locked up like two grizzly bears on their hind legs, growling, claws dug into each other, two alpha males in their prime. Except real grizzlies get to battle in the open, fresh, clean air, and we were in this stuffy, hot-ass gym. The next thing I knew, it was over. *Fweeet!* He had tried to pull a gut wrench on me, but we were sweaty and slippery, drenched in each other's perspiration, when I countered by turning him. I could always turn guys pretty well, and that's how I won with thirty seconds left in the match. *Fuck this gym, and fuck yeah. I'm a two-time Olympian,* I thought.

"Good job, Danny!" Bob said.

"That was a nice turn, Dan," my dad added.

That day was bittersweet. The two guys that had been there my whole career were able to see me find success once again, and Bob had been chosen as one of the Olympic coaches, but Randy and Heath had lost in their finals. I wished we could have all made the team together. Randy would always come so close (he was the number-one guy in 1997 and a semifinalist in 2000) but could never quite make it. Both of them would be in Atlanta as alternates, and this time it was their turn to be happy for me.

I was also given the chance to pass on the Olympic flame. A few weeks before the games started, when the Olympic torch and flame came in from Greece, it landed in Los Angeles, and I was one of the first people to run with it in Huntington Beach. Maybe that's what I needed to win gold. To hold the flame.

In 1996, the Olympic Village was at these brand-new, ten-story, state-of-the-art interior dorms that housed about ten thousand athletes. The Olympic Committee got hip to athletes hooking up, so condoms were handed out. I wasn't thinking about any late-night rendezvous. As soon as I got there, I tried to block out all the noise.

I was scheduled to compete the day after Opening Ceremonies, which meant I had to weigh in that day as well. Play time could wait. I needed my body in peak form, so I missed out on walking with my fellow Americans during the ceremony. I was in my room rehydrating after being depleted of water and fluids and needed all my energy for the next day. Still, I was able to watch the festivities on television, and although I wouldn't be able to run into Scottie Pippen again, Charles Barkley, or first-time Olympian Shaquille O'Neal, I would be able to wrestle at my best.

Before going to sleep, I wanted to watch the lighting of the giant torch. It was going to be hard to beat the Spanish archer in Barcelona, which is considered one of the greatest Olympic Ceremony moments. There was chatter about how the Atlanta Games flame would be lit, but the Olympic Committee did a good job at keeping it a mystery. I was about to doze off, when I watched the flame brought into the stadium. It was passed to former heavyweight boxing champion and Olympic bronze medalist Evander Holyfield, who lit the torch of Janet Evans, a four-time Olympic gold-medal swimmer, before bringing it up to the mystery person. The shadowy figure went to take the flame from Evans when the spotlight turned on him. The crowd roared when he was revealed.

There was, perhaps, the greatest boxer of all time—1960 light heavyweight gold medalist in Rome, Muhammad Ali.

For a second, I wished I was there to see it with my own two eyes. It was pretty badass to see an icon light the final torch. Ali's hands were grasping the torch firmly, although they were trembling due to his Parkinson's disease. The doctors say the blows to Ali's head and the damage he took in fights are what caused the disease, but as a warrior, that is the price one can pay. Today, the big talk is of CTE, a neurodegenerative brain disease, but I'll get to that later.

When I woke up the next day, I was focused and ready to win. There was only one way to show I was the best in the world—prove it. I had chopped off my mullet because I didn't want anyone grabbing my hair, and for these Olympics, one of the guys suggested we go bald for solidarity. That was fine with me. If I didn't need teeth, I sure as hell didn't need hair.

My first match was against three-time Olympian Pavel Frinta from the Czech Republic. In 1992, Pavel had come in eighth, two spots ahead of me, and even though I should've been on that podium, I knew what to expect from these Olympic refs and judges. It was a back-and-forth battle, but I was able to beat Pavel 3–1. The win put me in the winner's bracket, and I faced off against Sweden's Martin Lidberg about ninety minutes later.

I was familiar with Martin. We had beaten each other on the World circuit, and he was pretty strong. He'd go on to win the gold medal in the World Championships in 2003 and compete in two more Olympics, but on that day, I just wanted to get through him. The winner would get a bye in the next round and would be able to take the rest of the day off. It was a tough match, which could have gone either way, but he ended up winning 3–1, putting me on the brink of elimination. No bye and no rest for me.

That afternoon I took on Kyrgyzstan's Raatbek Sanatbayev. He was 1–1 like me, and the loser would be done. It was a double-elimination Olympic tournament. I never looked past an opponent, but I didn't have reason to be concerned. When we first clinched, I was able to feel his power and didn't think much of Raatbek. I knew he was another international wrestler from a country that was part of the old Soviet Union bloc. Not a big deal. I was used to this style. As the match continued, I could tell I was scoring points, but he was too. The match was close, but then I grabbed him, turned him for five seconds, and turned him again. *Okay, I'm ahead. He's not coming back from that.*

And having wrestled for twenty years, I had a general idea of the points being scored. I thought I was outscoring him when I grabbed him again. I didn't have the greatest hold but could've probably thrown him to score even more points. I decided not to because I didn't want to force it. I figured I had enough points and was ahead.

Fweeet! The whistled signaled the end of the match. I was ready to move on to Day Two. The ref grabbed our arms to lift the hand up of the winner. I had spent a lot of energy that day and was looking forward to having a good meal and preparing for my next opponent. But when the ref raised a hand up, it wasn't mine. *Something has to be wrong.*

"There's no way he beat you," Bob said as I went to the corner.

"I know," I said, pissed.

"Don't worry, Danny, we're going to protest this. We filmed it and have the proof."

In wrestling, there is limited replay if someone contests a match. Similar to instant replay in the NFL where a team wants to challenge a call, if video evidence clearly shows points were not awarded, the judges and ref can overturn the results of a match.

We had someone filming for us from the stands, and when they showed us the tape, the replay clearly showed I scored three points. The score should have been 5–3 in my favor, not 2–3. We brought the tape to the judges, but they refused to watch it. They only agreed to watch video recorded by the camera near the scorer's table. When they pulled up video from their angle, it was unclear whether I'd held him for five seconds. You could only see my back. We asked them again to watch our footage, which told a different story, but they waved us off. I had been eliminated once again.

I finished twelfth overall, a worse outing than my Olympic debut. Raatbek took eighth, Martin sixth, and Thomas Zander, who I lost to in '92, grabbed silver. Interestingly, Farkas didn't make it out of the second round, and I could only wonder what could've been in Barcelona.

Recently, I learned that Raatbek was running to become the head of the Kyrgyz Olympic Committee in 2006 (the previous leader had been murdered), but Raatbek never got the chance. When he was getting out of car at a shopping center, two guys assaulted him and one shot him in the head, killing him. It was shocking to learn someone I had respected and competed against had been murdered.

To drown my sorrows, I partied for fifteen days straight in Buckhead, the same area Randy and I had gotten into the altercation with the bouncers. Bar Atlanta took pretty good care of us Olympians. It was like the unofficial Olympic party spot. Athletes from other countries were there too, and though I'd have rather been competing, those were memorable times.

Due to my early exit, I had more time in Atlanta than Barcelona to watch other sports and was able to take in diving, boxing, gymnastics, track, and freestyle wrestling. It was cool to see other athletes at the top of their game, in their element, giving maximum effort on a huge stage. There seemed to be more media around since it was in the US. And although we aren't paid to be there, the Olympics had some big sponsors hosting events on a daily basis.

One of the sponsors promised a Jimmy Buffett performance during breakfast. I wasn't getting up early when I had gotten into party mode, but I've always liked his music, so I got up, probably still a bit drunk, and headed to the private event.

She looks familiar. It took me a second, but I knew I had seen her somewhere. It was Mary Lou Retton, the gold-medal gymnast. *That's kind of cool. Damn, my head still hurts. How many did I have last night?* I was there with Jason Gleasman, another American Greco guy, who wanted to see Jimmy as well. After thirty minutes, Buffett still hadn't shown up, so I wasn't going to stick around too much longer, especially on a few hours' sleep. I wasn't really aware of my surroundings; I just wanted to grab some food, listen to some music, and head out. As I was about to get up, I heard a female's voice next to me.

"Hey, how's it going?"

I turned, and sitting right next to me was Chelsea Clinton. *I can't be that fuckin' hungover. What is the president's daughter doing here?* "Oh, hey, how are you?" I said.

"I'm good. So, what sport do you compete in?" she replied.

"Wrestling." I didn't want to be rude, but my head was aching, and she probably had no idea what the fuck wrestling even was, outside of the fake shit.

"That's pretty cool. Some of my friends at school wrestle. What style do you compete in?"

Huh? This chick knows a little something. Damn. I was impressed to say the least. Most chicks at that time probably didn't even know who Hulk Hogan was. I told her I was a Greco guy and was even more surprised when she said, "So no going for the legs, right?"

"That's right."

I don't know if her knowing about wrestling made it better or worse for my head. I hadn't medaled, so there was nothing to write home to the president of the United States, er, her dad, about. And damn. No Jimmy Buffett. A no-show. Of course.

A few days after the Olympics, I went back to the White House. Some of the Olympians had their shiny medals adorning their necks. I didn't have shit. Disappointment once again.

Things had changed at the White House since the four years prior. The interior decor was different from the Bush administration, and I was half expecting a picnic luncheon again, but that wasn't the case. The air felt a little colder, and the mood much more formal.

Instead of Bush Sr. walking around shaking hands and having a laugh, we had to get in a line to take pictures with Bill, Hillary, and Chelsea. The visit wasn't as memorable; I don't even remember if we were served food. When it was my turn to take a picture with the Clintons, I saw Chelsea look at me, then whisper something to her mom. She asked me how I was doing, and we exchanged cordialities, then took the picture. I still have the photo. Maybe it was just a harmless glance, but you can see Chelsea looking down at my bulge.

★☆★

5.

ENTER THE DRAGON

I didn't grow up watching much television, but I can remember every few years there would be a film with some type of monster or dragon in it. It's the same shit, knight in shining armor picks up magical, massive sword, goes to some defunct castle, then slays the dragon to save the pretty princess.

Every time I went to war with my dragon, I always seemed to get engulfed in its flames or eaten up. The fucked-up thing was that I only got a shot at the dragon every four fuckin' years. I would be almost thirty for the next Olympics, and I still didn't have a career. I still had patience, but fuck, I couldn't keep trying to get a gold until I was fifty.

I was about to leave my house when my phone rang in the middle of May 1997.

"Hey, Dan."

"Hey, Randy, what's up?"

"I got this call from a fight promoter in Brazil. They're looking for another fighter at 175."

I had just won nationals in April to maintain my number-one status in USA Wrestling. I was still disappointed about Atlanta, but I had three more years until Sydney, and I was still getting better.

Randy had told me he had put in an application to fight in some mixed-martial-arts event for a promotion called the Ultimate

Fighting Championship (UFC) a couple months before, but they had passed him over.

"What do you think, Dan? I'm going to do it. We can make some extra cash."

I trusted Randy, so there wasn't much to think about. I was a two-time Olympian who couldn't afford my own place to live. I needed roommates because the $650 a month forced me to get help from my dad. The three years I wasn't number one, I made $350 a month as the number-two guy and $250 for being ranked third. No one was getting rich in the sport. Even the $2,500 stipend I received once a year from the Olympic Committee was gone within months. There were two years when the Olympic Committee felt generous and gave me a $2,500 bonus. That meant I was making between $6,700 to $12,800 a year after four years of blood, sweat, broken teeth, and brutal injuries to represent my country. I could have made more money working at McDonald's. More often than not, my dad would help me cover my bills so I could train. It wasn't looking any different as I was preparing for the 2000 Olympic Games. In other words, I was fucking broke.

"When is the fight?" I said.

"In a month in São Paulo. Travel and lodging will all be paid for."

It sounded cool, but what if it got in the way of my training? I wasn't dumb, though. I needed to start making money and didn't want to rely on my dad forever. I loved my dad but didn't want him paying for his grown-ass son who was struggling to make ends meet. That shit wasn't cool, and it wasn't going to change with the path I was on.

I had given more thought to a future career and applied to the Los Angeles College of Chiropractic after the Olympics. In my off time I had taken prerequisite chiropractic classes every Saturday and Sunday that were eight hours each day. Each class lasted a month. I had finally finished all the requirements and received a letter of acceptance into the program. I thought that would be a good occupation to get into, it was something that interested me. I'm good with my hands, chiropractors made good pay, and I'd had them working on me throughout my career. What more could I ask for from a job? I figured I could make a living from it and probably could come up with a good jingle for my business. "Go to Dr. Hendo where he'll break you, fix you, then crack your body into place."

"How much will I get paid?"

"It's tournament-style," Randy said. "For the first fight, you'll be paid three thousand dollars. You get another three thousand dollars for the second fight. They may give you a bonus after that, I don't know. I think it's a really good opportunity for us. We could go far in this caged fighting stuff."

Hmmm. I could prepare to go to chiropractor school full-time, which would limit some of my wrestling training regimen, or I could put school on halt and fight professionally for the first time. And, I wouldn't have to take out a loan for school, which would put me into debt. Even though I had no money, I didn't have any real debt. *Fuck going back to school.*

"Okay, I'll do it," I said.

"You're in?" Randy asked.

"Yeah, let's do it."

"I'll put you touch with Rico Chiapparelli, who's coordinating it."

I had competed in thousands of wrestling matches and trained countless hours since I was five years old. How different could a fight be? I figured it was like wrestling with submissions and some punching and kicking. I really didn't have a fuckin' clue.

Randy connected me with Rico, a former NCAA National Champion wrestler. He had formed the Real American Wrestling (RAW) team. Rico told me it would be me, Randy, and Tom "Big

Cat" Erikson heading to Brazil to fight. At 6'4" and over three hundred pounds, Tom was a physical specimen, a massive beast of a man. He was an American freestyle wrestler who had represented the United States and won the gold medal at the World Cup in 1992, and gold at nationals in 1997. He had started his MMA career less than a year earlier in November 1996, so this was new to all of us.

RIIIIIING—"Hello?"

"Hey, Dan." It was Randy.

"You still heading down here for training?" I asked.

"Not anymore. The UFC guys called me and want me to fight next week. I guess one of the heavyweights dropped out, and they want me to replace him."

We were supposed to fight June 15. If he was fighting at the end of May, there was no way he could turn around and fight two weeks later.

"Are you still going down with us to Brazil?"

"I don't think so. At least you'll have Rico and Tom there with you."

Since Randy's UFC fight was on short notice, I wasn't going to be able to head to Augusta, Georgia, for his MMA debut at UFC 13. But I knew Randy would be okay. He had won nationals with me in March and was the number-one guy again. There was nothing to worry about. I was right. Randy won the UFC Heavyweight Tournament by fighting twice in the same night, submitting his first opponent, and defeating the second one by TKO. Those were the days you fought multiple times in one night, which wrestlers were used to.

With two weeks until my first fight, I had to figure out a way to weigh in at 175 pounds. As an adult, I had never competed at 175. Even though my weight class was 180, my walk-around weight was about 200 pounds, give or take. That was me having food in my system and fully hydrated. I was used to cutting about twenty pounds before a match, but I always gave myself enough time to do so. I had mastered the art of wet cutting since I was in elementary school, so this was nothing new. What *was* new was that extra five pounds I had to lose. Cutting weight isn't fun, no matter how you do it, but to cut *five additional pounds*, having little fat to begin with, is daunting. At that point, muscle and water weight are being sacrificed to make it to the target weight. Since I was constantly training and competing in wrestling tournaments, my weight before the Brazil fight was already on the way down from 200. I was seventeen to twenty pounds away from my target, and I knew I had to work harder those next couple weeks to get that extra weight off.

I wasn't sure how I should prepare for the fight, so my training consisted of just wrestling. There were no MMA gyms in 1997. Sometimes I would hit the focus mitts with Rico a bit, but there were no sparring sessions or integration of Brazilian jiu-jitsu (BJJ). I wasn't a street fighter; every part of my combat routine had been calculated, focused, and intricate. I was a trained Greco-Roman wrestling assassin.

Rico told me my first opponent would be Crezio de Souza, a black belt in BJJ under the world renowned BJJ practitioner and fighter in his own right, Carlson Gracie. Carlson's black-belt students were fierce competitors and included future superstar Vitor Belfort, Murilo Bustamante, André Pederneiras, and Ricardo Libório.

In those early days, MMA tournaments were set up to pit different fighting styles against each other to see which martial art reigned supreme. Mixed martial arts organizations would have luta livres (Brazilian streetfighters), Brazilian jiu-jitsu practitioners, boxers, kickboxers, and fighters from different gyms like Chute

Box, Hammer House, and a handful of others compete against each other.

All of those arts were unique in the sense that they specialized in specific elements of hand-to-hand combat. The strikers, which included boxers, kickboxers, Muay Thai fighters, karate, and kung fu would have an advantage on their feet. Wrestlers would be able to take down their opponents and hold them down to try and punch their way to victory. Brazilian jiu-jitsu fighters would have the edge if they were able to grapple with their opponent and put them into a position where they could control and submit them.

All I knew about Crezio was that he was a world champion BJJ competitor and had a record of 1–1 in MMA. He had won his first match by submitting the other fighter with a rear naked choke, and in his second fight he had lost by TKO. Both fights were in Brazil against fellow Brazilians, and I would be the first American he would be facing—on his home turf.

As a wrestler, I knew facing someone with Crezio's skillset would mean that I had to be wary of submissions. In wrestling, the closest thing to a submission would be a pin, but in the fight, I knew anything could go. I was familiar with headlocks, but we couldn't choke our opponents or break their limbs. I had already said yes, so what did I have to lose?

I was excited when I boarded the plane at LAX with Rico and Tom. It was three days before the fight, and I had never been to Brazil. If you told me at the beginning of the year that I'd be heading to Brazil for a cage fight, I probably would've laughed at you.

Once we landed, we wanted to get started training, and I continued my weight cut right away. My mindset was to treat the fight like any other wrestling match. How do you even train for a fight with no fight trainers around yet?

When we first got there, it was an absolute clusterfuck. We were trying to figure out the lodging situation, where we could train, and other fight-week festivities. The gym that was allocated for me, Rico, and Tom to use was an hour away. That drive fuckin' sucked. We had to go out of our way to get our sessions in, and it ate away at our time to prepare. The language barrier didn't help either. As foreigners coming to fight Brazilians, we were not catered to by the locals. We proceeded as best we could.

My weight cut was progressing, but I still had a ways to go. I knew I could lose the extra five pounds but found myself wishing I had asked Randy to get this fight at a catch weight of 180 pounds. I had to cut out way more food and water than I was used to, and I began losing muscle mass.

As I prepared, I thought about the punches and kicks I might take. The thought of taking strikes to the head really didn't have much effect on me. I never thought about the pain I might endure. The year before, I had been competing with a wrestler from Israel, and he got so mad when I was beating his ass during our match, he took a swing and hit me in the face. I laughed. *That shit did not hurt.* I wasn't fazed at all. I knew from then on, I could take a punch. I just had to learn how to return the favor.

A couple days before the fight, I was in pretty good spirits. Then I learned that at a previous event there, one of the fighters had been stabbed by a fan. Apparently, during the match, a crazed fan rushed to the cage and knifed the fighter they didn't like through one of the cage hole openings. I was thinking, *They would never do this in the United States.* But this was Brazil, and *I* was beginning to realize I was in hostile territory.

After nearly passing out from starving and dehydrating myself, I made the weight cut down to 175. Immediately after, I rehydrated to try and get my body functioning properly again. I knew with the rough cut, I wouldn't be at full strength the next day, but I pushed all negative thoughts out of my mind. I couldn't go into the fight with a weak mindset. I looked at every situation positively, no matter what the fuck was going on. You can psyche yourself out into losing a battle before you even get there. When I faced off against wrestlers, I could tell if there was any doubt in their face. I knew I could break those guys quicker. One of the elements of war is to never show any doubt on your face. Keep your opponent guessing.

On fight day, I was in the locker room hitting the focus mitts with Rico and doing some wrestling warm-up exercises. *Breathe, Dan, breathe.* I didn't feel any nerves; those had gone away years ago when I first started wrestling. I had wrestled tens of thousands of hours of my life. What was there to be afraid of? Worst-case scenario, I get submitted or knocked out.

I made the first MMA walk of my career on June 15, 1997. The crowd booed at the top of their lungs as soon as I came out. *Fuck. Maybe I am a little nervous. What the fuck?*

I had become so used to being calm before a match that this nervousness was a shocker and a different feeling for me. I kept walking forward and saw my fate in front of me. *Wait, I'm about to get into that cage?*

This wasn't a wrestling mat. It was a human-sized, sawed-in-half birdcage that I was about to be locked up in. What an interesting concept. I quickly scanned my brain, thinking, *What other sports do athletes get locked up in a cage? Football? Nope. Not basketball. Baseball—no.* I thought about animals getting locked up in a zoo. *Inmates get locked up. And now, I'm about to be locked in.*

Since I was the challenger, I was the first to walk into the cage. I waited for what seemed like forever, but Crezio, a stocky, muscular Brazilian, finally started his walk out.

The crowd cheered as their hero made his way out. Brazilian fans cheer their own, especially when they are taking on a foreigner. It's home team or no team. When Crezio got in the cage, I was sure of it—for the first time in my adult life, I was nervous. After they locked the cage door, my mind got away from me for a second, and

I thought, *Fuck! What did I get myself into?* My mind started racing faster as the announcer made the introductions. Was I scared? Maybe. The feeling was so foreign to me, I really didn't know. I had been dominating opponents on the mat for so long that I had forgotten what it felt like to not have absolute confidence in my abilities and the outcome. Sure, I had lost occasionally, but I only lost to the best of the best. *Maybe this wasn't such a good idea.*

Time seemed to slow to a crawl as the ref brought us face-to-face to go over the rules. I felt absent, like I was watching myself outside of my body. It all changed in one fluid instant. As soon as the ref said, "Let's go," something clicked. I was back in the moment, and a man with every intention of dominating me was standing across the cage from me. All of my nervousness, hesitation, reservations, and fear vanished. This man wanted to hurt me, and only I could stop him. It was time to do battle and beat my opponent by putting my game plan into motion. It was time to let loose the dogs of war.

Crezio came forward right away and ducked down as I wound up and threw a right cross. He had his left arm up, which helped soften the blow, and he countered with a short left hook then a short right cross. *Yep, I got myself into a real fight.*

I felt the adrenaline flushing through my system, and I felt in the zone. I kept throwing punches, but I was ready to use my wrestling when I needed it.

He grabbed my waist looking to latch on. I turned to the right, changing levels on him and forcing myself away from his grasp, ready to scoot, scramble, or whizzer. I swung hard at his face with a right hook that glanced off his cheek. He threw back and it was two grapplers swinging wildly at each other. This was like a schoolyard fight, two untrained strikers trying to end the other's night or wobble them enough to go in for the kill.

A little later in the round, we finally locked up. He had one arm under me, and I had an arm under him. Crezio dropped to his knees and grabbed one of my legs, looking for a single-leg takedown. I sprawled back, thrusting both of my legs out to get a wide base. *Not today, Crezio.*

I didn't know much about jiu-jitsu, but I did know I didn't want to get tangled up with him on the ground. If he did that, he'd definitely have an advantage. Wrestlers are taught to never let anyone put you on your back. Being on your back opens you up to being pinned or scored against.

I was able to use my wrestling technique and strength to drive him back. I grabbed his legs and pulled them towards me with all of my might while I drove through him with my shoulders. I put him on his back and got into his half butterfly guard. Once on top of him, I tried to control him with one arm and punch with the other. Our heads came together, and I felt his chin digging into my eyeball. He wrapped his arms around my head to keep his chin piercing my eye socket. It felt like he was touching my brain with his chin. *Damn. That doesn't feel good.* His punches had no effect on me, but having Crezio's chin in my eye was surprisingly painful. *Just keep punching*, I told myself.

As I was trying to control him from the top, he was firing punches at me with his right hand, and then threw his legs up to get me off of him. I knew that being on top of him was the best position for me—that was something we had drilled in training—so I was being mindful of trying to hold that position.

While on the ground he was still on his back, but we had wriggled back and forth and ended up against the fence. He was defending while trying to use his position to get up. I kept punching with my strong hand, my right hand, and while it initially felt strange, it was becoming second nature. It was like I had done this a thousand times before.

My hands had always been strictly for grappling, but this new, higher, more intense form of combat had unleashed a different side of me. A ravenous killer instinct that I had used without punches my whole life. I had walked into the real-life *Enter the Dragon*, with different types of fighters trying to prove that their discipline was the best.

Crezio was one tough dude. Even with my punches sliding through his defenses, he was still fighting, still trying to hold on and use his strength to get the upper hand. Eventually, he was able to use his hips to get to a side position and finally use his right hand around me to get up. We got back to our feet. *C'mon, Dan, be dominant.*

Once on our feet, Crezio strutted forward and I arced a monster overhand right. The rotational force of my fist hurled towards his face, but he ducked, and my arm waved hi as it missed. *Damn. Well, at least I'm learning. Timing is everything.*

He grabbed me and we went down again. I scrambled like never before and ended up on top of him. The ref didn't seem to think either of us was doing enough so he stood us back up. Crezio wanted to make it a ground fight. He was looking to tie me up and take me down. He might have been a great BJJ practitioner, but my wrestling was canceling his takedown attempts.

I had watched boxing enough times to know what each punch was. I just wasn't good at it yet. I tried to throw one of Mike Tyson's signature uppercuts underneath Crezio's chin, but it missed. He wanted no part of the punches and started to back up. I threw another short uppercut and missed again. I feinted a straight right, and he backed up even more. My muscles had no practice of timing, so I was trying to land any way possible.

We tied up again, and this time he went on the offensive. Fighting wasn't exactly the same as wrestling. My brain didn't have enough data to have a counter to every move. So out of nowhere, I threw a right knee at his face that missed. I had never thrown a knee in my life, but it was instinctual. That would've been an automatic disqualification in wrestling.

I backed up to create enough separation to get my balance back. Crezio started to come forward, and after another one of my punches missed him, he put one arm around my leg and one around my waist and drove me forward. This time he was able to finish the takedown and put me on my ass. Crezio then used his BJJ to his advantage. He jumped his legs over me and managed to get a full mount position. *Fuck, this is not what I wanted.* I turned my back to try and sweep him off of me, but he had a strong base. I wasn't sure if he was taking anything extra to give him a power boost, but he was a Carlson Gracie black belt.

After failing to sweep him, I definitely didn't want him taking my back. In wrestling training we never drilled submission defenses, especially from the back. I just knew I needed to get the fuck out of that position. He mounted me again, and I was like a fish out of water, flailing, trying to get my orientation back. He started throwing punches, but surprisingly, none of them hurt. But I wasn't trying to stay in that same position either.

I was finally able to use my wrestling and strength to twist him and turn him over. I muscled it more than anything. I got on top of him, this time in full guard, and started throwing punches down. I had been missing a fuckload of punches, but finally, some of them were finding their mark. I kept throwing, hammering his face and body.

Crezio put his hands up to defend the punches, then he used his knees as a barrier and tried to keep some separation between us. I could see he wasn't hurt by my barrage. My punches seemed to be going across, around, and everywhere except my target—his face. After a few more errant punches, I felt the ref pull me off Crezio. *What just happened?*

I was stunned. I backed up and wasn't sure what the fuck was going on. I could hear Portuguese but didn't understand a word. Maybe they were going to stand the fight back up? I could see Crezio was hurt, but his bearings were all there.

The ref said something to him, and Crezio immediately started to protest. With a break in the action, I could hear the crowd clearly. They started booing and throwing shit into the cage. *Ah, shit.* Thoughts of the stabbed fighter crept into my mind. *Being locked in isn't so bad,* I thought. I still didn't know what was going on, but my legs started to cramp up from the tough weight cut. I went to my corner and sat down. At least the fence could keep some shit from hitting me.

When I had watched the first televised mixed martial arts fight, I didn't recall the crowd being hostile. In fact, none of the videos I watched had crowds throwing shit. Cage fighting was still in its infancy, with UFC 1 taking place only four years earlier in 1993.

There were only three rules at the time—no biting, eye gouging, or groin shots. Everything else was fair play. The sport was heavily criticized in America for the lack of rules and what many deemed to be too brutal. Lawmakers were calling to abolish the sport, and Senator John McCain labeled it "human cockfighting." The sport's future was uncertain as politicians like McCain, who was an advocate for boxing, were fighting to have sanctioned fighting banned and encouraged Americans to boycott the UFC and promotions like it.

Seeking to get more recognition as a real and regulated sport, the UFC and other organizations began introducing more rules in an attempt to become legitimate. Fighter health and safety became more of a priority, which meant referees stopped fights when they deemed a fighter to be too hurt. At times, that led to early stoppages, and in my career, I would come out on the fucked-up end of fights stopped early. But human error is part of the sport.

The referee called me and Crezio over and said he was going to declare me the winner. He had stopped the fight and was adamant that there would be no restart; Crezio's protest was for naught. The ref raised my hand, and the announcer declared me the winner as more boos echoed throughout the arena. Crezio was a good sport and true martial artist when he grabbed the mic, and, in Portuguese, told the crowd to settle down and respect the referee's decision. I'd be moving on to the finals. If he would have stayed pissed off, I have no doubt it would have incited a riot. Instead of my first MMA win, I might have become a news headline: *Two-time American Olympian Stabbed After Cage Fight in Brazil.*

I waited about an hour and a half in the locker rooms before I entered the cage again for the finals. I was happy that my opponent would be an American. The Brazilians could have cared less which American kicked the other's ass, so at least there would be no bullshit after the fight.

Ironically, I was pitted against another wrestler, Eric Smith. Eric was a two-time All-American out of Ohio State, who was bigger and much more muscular than me. He was fighting out of the famed Team Hammer House, led by then-current UFC Heavyweight Champion Mark Coleman. Mark was also an early MMA pioneer and had won the UFC 10 and UFC 11 tournaments a year earlier. He would also go on to win the Pride Fighting Championships 2000 Open Weight Grand Prix. The UFC would induct him in their Hall of Fame in 2008, and his team also produced early stars like future UFC Heavyweight Champion Kevin Randleman and Phil Baroni.

I knew my fight with Eric would be far different than my battle with Crezio. I didn't have to worry about being strangled or

Eric breaking one of my limbs, and it helped I had gotten that first fight out of the way.

When I made my second walk to the cage, the nervousness from ninety minutes prior had dissipated. I had no second thoughts or doubt. It was just another fight to me, another opportunity to get better at hand-to-hand war.

When the ref yelled, "Let's go," we walked towards each other, and Eric started to circle to his right, so I did the same. We had both of our hands up, like two Rock 'Em Sock 'Em Robots before they start pounding each other.

Eric circled back to his left, and this time, I stayed my ground, waiting to make contact. Less than ten seconds later, Eric rocketed forward and blasted a right hand at the same eye Crezio's chin had dug into, but he only brushed it, and the momentum pushed me back into the cage.

My right hand touched the steel bars, and Eric rushed again, throwing wild robotic punches towards my face. I hurled a left hook at his face that made him step back and take the center of the cage. I moved to my left and was ready to punch mano-a-mano, but he shot in for a double-leg takedown. I was ready. I sprawled and put my left arm around his neck, which in wrestling would be a front headlock, then put my right arm inside his left arm to lock in an arm-in guillotine. I then wrapped my legs around his and started to arch my back. I knew I had a solid choke on him, and I wasn't letting go for anything. I was like a pit bull, jaws locked with a death grip.

Eric tried to grab my right leg for a split second, but the choke was too tight. I could feel his air starting to leave him as he slowly started to go down. He fell backwards with me, and the choke sunk in deeper. I had an extremely strong grip from wrestling and strength from the years of Bob's workout routine. Eric was on his back and on the verge of going to sleep. The ref tapped my back to end the fight, and when I let go, he was completely out. The ref pushed him on the chest, and then took out his mouthpiece as I walked away. When he regained consciousness, he didn't know that I had put him to sleep. He tried to get back into the fight, but his teammate, Kevin Randleman, was there to calm him down and let him know what had happened.

I had won the tournament, but there was little celebration from me. I put my hands up for a few seconds, then again momentarily when the referee raised my hands. I was glad that I had won, made some money, but I had done it for a payday. I had no dreams of greatness in mixed martial arts. I just didn't want to keep asking my dad for money.

The promotion awarded me a big, shiny gold cup. It was as if I could win gold in every other tournament but couldn't get in striking distance of an Olympic gold medal. I had three years until the 2000 Olympics. Even though I had written off school, I wasn't a fool. I kept the acceptance letter because I was still unsure of my future. Wrestling was life, but I knew I would need a new beginning in something else at some point soon. I just didn't know what that new thing was.

☆☆☆

6

UFC FIRST-TIMER | GOING FOR BLOOD

Fighting can be like a beautiful woman, or ugly like a street tramp. When done with grace and style, you can get lost in a match and captivated, just like a woman's beauty. If you watch a fight with little technique, wild punches, or stalling tomato cans, it's like the street lady you don't want anything to do with.

I may have not been a street rat trying out the fighting thing, but I certainly wasn't a ninja either. The art of war is learned, not born into.

"Hey Dan, it's Rico."

"What's up?"

"You ready for another fight?"

That was a great question. In April 1998, I lost my number-one status after not placing first at nationals. I had maintained my top ranking by winning in 1997, but I'd had a bad tournament. The margin of error is minute at that level; one mistake and your opponent's hand gets raised.

"Is it in Brazil again?" I didn't want to go back there so quickly. Traveling to Brazil and back would take time away from training. I had two years until the 2000 Olympics and had my eyes set on making the team for a third time. Gold medals adorned my house, but I was desperate to win an Olympic gold, wrestling's Mount

Rushmore. I have always been a patient person, but I was anxious. I needed gold to fulfill me.

"It's in Alabama," Rico answered back.

Whew. I don't have to worry about thirty hours of travel time. Fighting did have some instant perks. USA Wrestling had again lowered my pay, but I didn't need to rely on my dad for money as much. I was paid $3,000 to show up and fight in Brazil, $3,000 for my second fight, and a bonus of $6,000 for winning the tournament. A grand total of $12,000, which was about the same amount I was making per year as an Olympic wrestler. Not bad for one night of work.

"How much are they going to pay me?"

Rico said, "Five thousand dollars for the first fight, and if you beat him, another five thousand dollars. They said they'll throw in a bonus if you win it."

At that time, the only reason I fought was to fund my wrestling. I really didn't care about getting in a cage. I wasn't thinking about being a world champion or any type of MMA legacy. I was trying to figure out the trajectory of my life after wrestling. I didn't want to go back to school. "Alright, class, get out your notebooks and scantrons for a pop quiz." Fuck that. I wouldn't mind a secretary coming to my office to say, "Doctor Henderson, your patient needs you in Room Three." But going back to school did not appeal to me. I'd rather fight and get paid than have to listen to a couple more years of lectures.

"Yeah, I'll do it; when is it?"

"Next month. May fifteenth. It'll be in the two-hundred-and-under weight class in the UFC."

I had watched the UFC long before Randy's first fight with the promotion. I had seen videos of UFC fights starting with the first one in 1993. Behemoth-looking men would get in the cage and fight guys in other disciplines, some who were much smaller, and prove which martial art was best. I always thought mixed martial arts was something I could do, I just didn't know how my size and wrestling would cross over.

I *was* intrigued by some of the smaller guys like Royce Gracie. He would fight guys that outweighed him by a hundred pounds. I found that to be truly impressive. In wrestling, if you had an opponent that was ten to twenty pounds heavier, that person would have an enormous advantage. That's why there are weight classes. When all things are equal in wrestling, the larger person wins. The same could be said about mixed martial arts.

Once Randy and I started fighting, our careers seemed to parallel in many ways. In 1997, Randy had two more fights in the UFC. I cornered and traveled with him for both. The first was in Mississippi at UFC 15 where he TKO'd a young Vitor Belfort who had muscles the size of a Mack Truck. Next, we went to Japan, where Randy wore wrestling shoes and tights and won the UFC Heavyweight Championship by beating Maurice Smith. We wore the same thing in training that we were wearing in our fights. We were merely wrestlers trying our hand at fighting to pay our bills.

The airplane wheels touched down in the Deep South. It was the first time I had been to Alabama. As soon as I got out of the plane, I felt the humidity hit my skin like a grimy, salty shower. The smell was much different from what I was used to in California, but it wasn't overly bothersome. But I wasn't there to sightsee or for the aesthetics. My sole purpose was to win the UFC 17 Middleweight Tournament.

I was surprised how empty and rural Mobile was. Half of the businesses on Main Street had been boarded up. Five-foot-long weeds covered the front yards of the smaller houses there, and they looked like they hadn't been lived in for years. I was surprised how a few people recognized me. They had watched some of my Olympic matches and had no idea I was in town to fight.

On fight day, I threw on a pair of four-ounce gloves and started hitting pads with Rico. We had been in town for a few days, and we still hadn't figured out how to properly train for an MMA fight. Me and Randy would do some wrestling drills and slam some punches on the heavy bag. Occasionally, there would be times when I faced off against Randy, and we would throw rabbit punches at each other's faces and bodies, but nothing close to what our sparring would become.

The UFC was not yet owned by Zuffa (Fertitta brothers and Dana White), and mixed martial arts was on shaky ground in the US. The sport was highly scrutinized and still getting backlash from politicians. The commissioner at the time, Jeff Blatnick, wanted to change the narrative. A former Greco-Roman Olympic gold medalist, Jeff knew the sport was on the fringe of being barred. At our fighter meeting before UFC 17, Jeff told us (and later the media) that the competition would no longer be referred to as "no holds barred." The new term would be "mixed martial arts," which he deemed more graceful terminology. (Jeff unfortunately passed away in 2012, and I don't think he got enough credit for helping keep the sport legal. I highly doubt there would be expensive multi-million-dollar UFC facilities like the Apex or Performance Institute without him.)

Damn. There's quite a few people here. When I made the walk out to the cage, I was surprised by the crowd size. The venue looked pretty full, with about five or six thousand people in attendance. I wasn't the only newcomer to the promotion. The card included: Jeremy Horn, Carlos Newton, who would become the UFC Middleweight Champion, and future UFC Hall of Famer and two-time UFC Light Heavyweight Champion Chuck Liddell. There were also UFC veterans like Tank Abbott, who started at UFC 6, former UFC Heavyweight Champion Mark Coleman, and the UFC Light Heavyweight Champion at the time, Frank Shamrock.

For my first fight, I was matched up against Brazilian jiu-jitsu practitioner, Allan Góes, a Carlson Gracie black belt. Allan was an eight-time national jiu-jitsu champion, and even though this was going to be his fifth MMA fight, he claimed to have had 250 unsanctioned fights in his career. Whatever the case was, the dude had more fighting experience than me.

"Okay, Dan, you know his game. You know what to do." Randy was giving me some last pointers as Allan made the walk to the cage wearing his gi. "Don't get on your back, and don't let him take your back." I nodded my head. *Focus, Dan.*

Even though I already knew the shit Randy was saying, it was good to get that reinforcement. Randy was the heavyweight champ, but we didn't win any of our fights from our backs. As a child, I was taught by my dad, "Don't get put on your ass or your back, Dan." Wrestlers who ended up in that position didn't get very far. Brazilian jiu-jitsu was far different. Those guys were used to being on their backs submitting their opponents with a wide array of finishes in their tool belts.

"And weighing in at 193 pounds. Fighting out of Huntington Beach, California, fighting with the RAW Team, please welcome... Dan Henderson!"

This was the very first time the ring announcer, Bruce Buffer, or the "Veteran Voice of the UFC," would announce my name. He was just Bruce back then. Who would have thought he'd be the last one to announce my name twenty years later for my final fight?

Please don't get put on your fuckin' back, I told myself as I stared at Allan across the cage. The ref gives me the cue. "Are you ready?" I nod my head. *Yep, I sure am.* "Are you ready?" Allan gives a nod. "Get busy!" With that, the ref clapped his hands, and I met Allan at the center of the cage.

Blam! Allan put his head down and threw an overhand right that caught me flush on my jaw and dropped me. *Whoops. I didn't see that coming.* I was learning mixed martial arts in real time. If a move didn't seem to work, then I would try something different. In wrestling, there is no action if you don't go forward, so I tried that approach with Allan.

I marched towards him and grabbed his leg. I had seen some leg submissions before but had never tried them out. *Fuck it.* I went for a heel hook that would've ended the fight by submission or breaking his fuckin' leg. It didn't work, but I got up and went back to punching. I threw some wild George Foreman-esque punches that mostly missed the mark.

We continued to fight for almost nine minutes without a break when—*SPLAAAAT! Fuck.* He dropped me on my ass, then—*CRAAAAACK!* I felt his shin go right into my forehead. He soccer-kicked the fuck out of me. The next few seconds were a blur. I remember putting my hands around the referee's waist. *What the fuck just happened,* I thought.

The referee had stopped the action because soccer kicks had been deemed illegal in the UFC. When I got up, it was still unclear of what the fuck was going on. I put my hands up in protest because I thought he stopped the fight. There were murmurs from the crowd, whistling and groaning then the slow sound of boos, which grew to a crescendo, and chants from the crowd saying, "bullshit, bullshit, bullshit." I went to my corner when the ref, Joe Hamilton, talked it over with "Big" John McCarthy, who was helping officiate from outside the cage.

The outcome was a warning for Allan, but no point deduction. If the fight were today, it would've been called off. I'm glad it wasn't, because I wanted to keep fighting. We eventually went to overtime where I was finally able to impose my will on Allan and dropped him with those wild uppercuts I had been practicing. They were not accurate, but when they finally landed, he felt them.

The fight went the distance, and I was awarded a decision victory. I had won another fight.

I didn't have time to gloat. An hour later, I was matched up against Carlos Newton, who'd won his fight by submission in under a minute. *Damn. This fucker is going to be fresh as an ox.*

Boom! I immediately got caught with a right hand and dropped to one knee. *Here we go again.* The referee, Big John, dashed in, then backed off after I grabbed Carlos and finished a double-leg takedown to slam him down. But Carlos was strong and the fresher fighter, which helped him get up soon after.

I decided to try and assault him with punches. *Fwooomp, fwoomp.* I threw some right crosses and tried to take his head off. I wasn't going the Floyd Mayweather route. I was throwing Joe Frazier and Rocky Marciano bombs. I wanted *blood*, so I could finish Carlos. He was trying to do the same thing to me.

In the overtime round, Carlos was able to weather my violent storm, and he threw a right cross that connected square with my left jaw. *Damn. That didn't feel right.* I took a step forward, and he landed a knee that put me off balance. I slipped down to the mat. He rushed forward and I did a somersault to get him on his back, but when I put my chin on his chest to get a better position, something weird happened. *Oh shit. Why the fuck is my jaw moving?* Something was wrong. I felt like the bones around the upper part of my jaw had detached from my jawbone itself. My skin was the only thing holding it in place.

I wasn't going to quit or bitch about it, so I continued on trying to win the fight any way I could. I was able to take Carlos down and ground and pound him until the end of the round. I wasn't able to finish him, but I had given it my all. The two fights had been grueling. I won by split decision, and Bruce Buffer announced me UFC Middleweight Tournament Champion.

The CEO of SEG (which owned the UFC at the time) and co-founder of the UFC, Bob Meyrowitz, awarded me a medal and hung it around my neck. Bob congratulated me, and then a twenty-nine-year-old Joe Rogan interviewed me. He asked about a potential fight with Frank Shamrock, who was the UFC Middleweight Champ. I told Joe my only focus was *wrestling*. Nothing more, nothing less.

I was just happy I had gotten the bonus for winning the tournament. The $22,000 payday meant I wouldn't have to ask my dad for grocery money or all the other shit he helped me out with. It was the most money I'd ever made at once, but I felt every minute of those fights in my body. That blood money was earned. In wrestling, I wasn't taking punches, elbows, or kicks.

After the fight, my adrenaline started to wear off, and I knew something was wrong. My jaw was fuckin' hurting even more. There would be no afterparty of free booze following my wins in Mobile. I wouldn't be turning up or making it rain dollar bills at some dimly lit nightclub. Not that I would have done that anyways. My idea of a good party was some vodka, tequila, or brews with country music at a local bar. But that was the furthest thing from my mind. I needed to go get my shit checked out.

Me and my brother Tom at 2 and 4 years of age.

A 10-year-old me in the middle of a shoulder throw at a wrestling tournament.

Nationals Team Championship (1987) my dad top row second from left and Bob Anderson next to him.

Tom and me jumping rope in front of the van.

Getting my start in wrestling, probably 5 or 6 years old.

Dad, Tom, Me, Mom, Dad's mom (Dee) and dad (Bill). Christmas, sophomore year in high school.

In seventh grade wrestling Greco-Roman and scoring points with a gut wrench on my opponent.

My lone high school match against Tom. It was a high scoring match where he beat me 16-15.

A folkstyle match in high school doing a crotch lift.

Senior year 1988, Junior Nationals
Championship.

Taking first place in
Junior Olympics, July 1991

Winning the Rings King of Kings Tournament and banking my first
major paycheck.

My second trip to the White House with the Clintons running the country.

At UFC 100 weigh-ins, getting ready for my faceoff with Michael Bisping.

In fight camp getting ready for my next opponent.

At my 2022 Annual Pig Roast with Randy Couture and my brother-in-law Chris Pendleton.

Bellator CEO Scott Coker got some legends together for Fedor's last fight February 2023 in LA to honor us. From l. to r. Royce Gracie, Matt Hughes, Chuck Liddell, Randy Couture, me, and Chael Sonnen.

My family circa 2013. From l. to r. Sierra, me, Daniella, my wife, Rachel, Sophia, and Reese.

Me, Dad, and my brother Tom in Lake Tahoe, 2011.

From left to right: Craig Morgan, Randy Couture, me, and LOCASH at a country music event.

This photo and top photos on insert page 6 courtesy of James Morrey.

☆☆☆
7

JAW WIRED SHUT | OLYMPIC GOLD?

After the fight, I skipped the hotel and went to what seemed to be the only open hospital in Mobile that night. I wasn't going to whine about my injury; hell, my dad probably would've just put some string around my mouth and jaw to fix it, but I wanted to know what was wrong with my jaw before I went back to California.

"Sorry, Mister Henderson. We're going to need you to come back for another X-ray."

"Why do you need another one?" I asked the nurse. She beckoned me to follow her for what seemed to be the hundredth time into the imaging room. "I'm sorry, dear, the doctor said the last ones came back inconclusive."

It felt like I was at the hospital forever. I wasn't a fan of hospitals, there was nothing that resembled an afterparty, no booze or music to celebrate. Instead I was met with a cold, bleak building, with indoor lights turned on 1000 percent, shining down on you from every square ceiling panel. *Like, what the fuck?* Who wants to be in a place of death?

Creeeeeak, the door opened, and this time it was a doctor.

"Mister Henderson, I looked at the new X-rays, and I can't see if it's broken or not." *These guys are fuckin' incompetent as fuck,* I thought.

"Doc, that's what everyone else has been saying, but my shit is hurting a bit more. Can you at least give me a painkiller?"

The doctor looked like he was working his fifth graveyard shift in a row. He had a patchy beard, and his white coat had a tint of beige. "Unfortunately we can't until we determine if it's broken. We're going to have to take another look and take another X-ray."

I guess he wanted me to suffer with him on this shift. The nurses X-rayed me at least ten more times before they gave me a painkiller. It was like I was asking them for crack or the secret code to nuclear weapons. The doctor wanted his last say and came back one more time.

"Don't take the painkillers when you're not supposed to or when you don't have any pain. They can be highly addictive. And when you get back to California, make an appointment with your doctor to get a second opinion. Maybe they can tell you if it's broken or just bruised."

When I got back to the Golden State, I went to a specialist to see why my jaw still felt like Jell-O. Due to the clueless emergency room doctors in Alabama, I was initially skeptical about the specialist in California. I didn't want to do a hundred more X-rays and have them come back inconclusive.

"Your jaw is definitely broken and dislocated. You're going to need surgery," the specialist said. "We're going to have to wire it shut to let it start healing ASAP."

Shit, this sucks, but at least he knows what he's doing. The next day, the doctor performed the surgery by adding a metal plate and wired my jaw shut like I was Robocop. I wasn't a big talker, but now I had no choice but to completely shut the fuck up.

"We're going to need you to come back in two days, so we can make sure it's healing properly. Remember, try to not move your mouth too much."

For the next couple days I went on a straw diet. It sucked ass, and at times I would get an itch in an area where the wire was at but couldn't touch. Those will drive you crazy. And I started to drop in weight. I could've done an infomercial.

"Want to lose weight quickly? Get your fuckin' jaw wired shut and go on a straw diet. It's a quick way to slim down and get your grumbling stomach that lean look you've always wanted."

When I went back to the specialist, they checked to see if my jaw was healing properly but left the wire on. Apparently, it wasn't ready to come off yet. I felt along my face and jawline to see how bad the pain was. It was bearable, but more importantly, I couldn't wait to eat real food.

"I just took a look at the new X-rays, and for some reason, your jawbone has come out of the socket again," the doctor said.

"What the fuck?" I mumbled, partly because I was shocked, but mostly because I hadn't opened my mouth in a couple days.

"We're going to have to wire it again and do surgery on it to help it connect back in place. We'll leave the wire on for ten days, then do the surgery right after."

Fuuuuck. Back to my straw diet. In those ten days, I lost another ten pounds of muscle before I went under the knife. They were able to successfully connect the jaw to the bone socket, and I thought that was the end of that. It wasn't. The incision had gotten infected, and I spit out a half a cup of pus, which was draining from the inside of my mouth. It was fuckin' disgusting. You definitely don't want to ever experience an infection inside of your mouth. The doctors put me on a new dose of antibiotics. Then came even more shitty news when I went back to the specialist.

"Dan, I hate to say this, but your jawbone is dislocated again."

I hate to say this. Anytime you hear someone preface what they're about to say with this line, it's like, don't fuckin' say it then. And how the hell did the wire *and* surgery not work?

The doctor continued, "If you see here, it's your muscles that are pulling the jawbone out of your socket. Honestly, I haven't seen this before. Your muscles are so tight and dense, we're going to have to do a second surgery to put it back in place."

Two surgeries in two months. This shit better work. Thirty days after the surgery, the same thing happened. The muscles in my body pulled the jaw out of alignment once again. They said I was going to need a third surgery. I wasn't going for it.

"I'll pass, Doc," I said. "Leave it like it is."

The doctor looked confused. "What? Your jaw is out of whack. It needs to heal by putting it in the right spot."

"It's all good, Doc. I'll be fine. Thank you though."

With that, I walked out of the office. I was done with surgeries. I didn't care that my jaw looked like Frankenstein. I figured it could heal itself, which it did. The muscles near my mouth, cheek, and around the jaw started to build up scar tissue to make its own socket for my jawbone. It didn't heal properly, but I wasn't hindered by it too much. I just needed it to be stable. There were times when I would get hit in the right spot with an uppercut to my jaw. That's when I could feel my jaw move around a little bit in the makeshift socket my muscles made. It happened a few times in my career, but not often. Even when I spar today, I don't really notice it.

The surgeries and recovery hindered my training for a few months in 1998, but I still had a ton of wrestling to do. I had already medaled five times that year, including two gold medals, but I had my eyes set on the 1998 Greco-Roman Pan American Championships. There was a Cuban wrestler I wanted to test myself against who was three years younger than me but who was quickly rising as one of the best Greco guys out there.

The Cubans had boycotted the 1984 and 1988 Olympics, but when they started back in 1992, they were pretty fuckin' good. The tiny island country took home five medals in Barcelona, three in Atlanta, and were a force to be reckoned with internationally in both Greco and freestyle.

Luis Enrique Méndez was the Cuban my target was on at those Pan Am Championships. I had won silver in the 1994 Championships, bronze at the 1995 Pan American Games (not to be confused with the Pan Am Championships, the Games are held once every four years and usually the year before the Olympics), and wanted to face a guy I might see in the 2000 Olympic Games. But I never got a chance to wrestle him that year. In the semifinal match, which would have put me against Luis, bullshit Olympic-type politics came back.

I was wrestling against a Mexican wrestler who I had never seen or heard of. In the first five seconds of the match, I clubbed him in the head with my bicep as I went to sink in a headlock. I put him on his back and was awarded three points right away. I was wrestling this no-name aggressively so I could get to the finals unscathed. But as soon as I did that, the motherfucker started complaining to the ref about his neck hurting, and the Canadian ref put a halt to the match.

"Why are we stopping?" I asked the ref.

"Hold on. Go over there," he said, pointing a few feet away.

The ref went over to check on my opponent who continued the act and was holding on to his neck like I'd tried to saw it off. The ref talked it over with the judges and came back to me and said, "Hey, Henderson, it's over, you're being disqualified for an illegal move." *What in the fuck?*

"When is a headlock an illegal move?" I asked. I was fucking pissed.

He snapped back, "You did the move too hard, that's why it's illegal."

Never in my wrestling career had I heard some bullshit like this. *Let me think about this. I did a legal move too hard? Nope, not mak-*

ing a connection to this bullshit. I've never heard of a sport where you can do a legal move too hard. There would be immense backlash from that. But we didn't have the same oversight major sports did. Wrestling was a sport with Wild West regulation.

The Mexican went on to face Luis in the finals but decided to forfeit the match due to his alleged injury. Instead of letting me face off with the Cuban, I was awarded bronze, Luis took gold, and the beta took silver. The Mexican bragged about having a bye his first match and needing only five seconds of mat time to take second place. It was at that point I knew the sport was getting far more political.

I got a call from Rico a few months later saying that the UFC had made an official offer for me to fight Frank Shamrock in Brazil. It would be for Frank's middleweight championship belt in São Paulo. He had been in MMA longer than me with five times the number of fights, but I was more attuned to the pay. My body was banged up that year with the fights and after competing in over a dozen wrestling tournaments across the globe. If I was serious about the Olympics, I needed more wrestling training and a rest from fighting. And I wasn't able to enhance my skills when my jaw was fucked up. The price had to be right to fight.

"How much are they offering?" I said.

"Well, that's the thing. They're offering less for this title fight than for your tournament win. They're doing the same thing to Randy."

The UFC was still having issues with adapting the sport to mainstream America. It was banned in many states, and they had lost some of their cable contracts due to pressure by local lawmakers. Their final offer was $10,000, contingent on me beating Frank. If I lost, the money was half.

"I know it's not a guarantee, but that's their final offer," Rico said. "Randy's going to vacate his title as well. I got him more money to fight in Japan. I think that's where the real money is. I'm going to try and get you a deal for more money out there too."

I would have accepted the deal if the $10,000 was guaranteed and they threw in a win bonus, but the UFC didn't have the money to put up, and it wasn't going to be worth the wrestling sacrifice. And I wasn't intrigued with the belt being on the line. At the time, it had little importance to me and was never a goal of mine. Plus, I was still able to live off the tournament money. It wasn't like I was a big spender. I knew how to budget money to make it last. All I needed were the bare necessities: food, a place to sleep, and transportation. What more does an Olympic-minded wrestler need? I had all three.

RIIIIING. RIIIII—I pick up my new cellular phone. It was Rico.

"I got you a deal in Japan, Dan. It's better than what the UFC offered."

"How much are they offering? And when would it be?"

The MMA scene in Japan was much bigger than in the United States. The Japanese had latched on to it quickly, because they had come up with a shoot-style wrestling where two wrestlers, who had a fanbase, would battle against each other using wrestling techniques along with punches, kicks, and submissions. It was a precursor to mixed martial arts, and the Japanese fans loved and appreciated it. Even though wrestling goes back thousands of years, martial arts in Asia also goes back centuries. They were the ones that first brought it to Brazil.

There was a Japanese native, Mitsuyo Maeda, who went down to Brazil to teach the original Gracies, Carlos and Hélio Gracie, jiu-jitsu, and they started to slowly evolve it into modern-day

Brazilian jiu-jitsu. I would have many battles with Brazilians. Also in Japan, from the 1100s to 1876, their samurais would battle with a sword to the death, which the phrase "death before dishonor" was coined for. That may be why MMA found a rapid ascent in Japan. And the fiercer and more brutal the fighter, the more the crowd adored him. That's why promotions had more money to pay fighters. Fans were doling out the cash.

"The fight will be sometime in the next few months," Rico said. "It's for this promotion Rings. I'm still figuring out the final numbers with them because I'm doing a deal for Randy as well."

I thought, *Okay. No problem. We're all on the same team.* Me and Randy had never fought on the same card together, but that would be cool. We had cornered each other for just about every fight, so it would've made it easier on our schedules.

"Yeah, I'm in. I'm good to go whenever. Just let me know when."

Whenever money is involved, so is greed, whether it's someone greasing an official's hand in wrestling, or trying to make a buck off a fighter. I was never taught to be anything but forthcoming and honorable growing up. My dad wouldn't have it any other way. Bob was the same way too. His goal was to help kids be better wrestlers in hopes of one day getting them into the Olympics. And it worked. Did he want anything in return? Nope. Unfortunately, that wasn't the case with Rico.

In 1997, I had made a few connections in Japan while I was out there cornering for Randy. One of my contacts was familiar with Rings and the other Japanese promoters. I had asked him a question about Rings, and that is when I caught wind that Rico was using me as leverage to get Randy more money to go to Rings. He had already vacated his UFC heavyweight title when they couldn't come to an agreement, and ended up fighting in another Japanese promotion, Vale Tudo Japan, a few months prior in October 1998.

Apparently, I was a pawn for Rico and his deceitful negotiations. If they didn't pay Randy more money, they weren't going to get me, which meant more money for him. As a friend, I was all for Randy getting paid a lot; hell, I want all fighters taken care of, but Rico wasn't trying to get an increase for me, which was total bullshit. He was already getting 20 percent of my purse; it wasn't like I was pocketing everything I made. I cleared less than $25,000 of the $34,000 I made for the four fights in two years. If you split it up, I only made $12,500 per year for 1997 and 1998. The money was nothing to write home about. I decided to give Rico a call.

"Hey, Dan, what's up?"

"I know you're using me to get more money for Randy. It's all good, but I just wanted to let you know, from here on out, I'll deal with Rings, and we can just go our separate ways."

He sounded caught off guard, saying, "Uh. I mean, yeah, but just let me handle it. I'll get you more money too."

You only get one chance with me. "No, I just want out of the contract, Rico. I'll be able to handle it myself."

Rico eventually agreed to let me out of the deal, which I thought was the end of that. I went back to my contact, the Japanese guy (who was kind of like a manager), and paid him to negotiate a deal with Rings. We did most of our communication over email, which wasn't the normal way to conduct business back then, but the deal got done; I had a fight date. October 28, 1999, in Tokyo.

Even though Randy and I were still looking for Olympic glory, we agreed to incorporate MMA practice after our wrestling training ended. If we were going to continue to fight, our skill levels needed to increase if we didn't want to lose.

In March, Randy had his sixth MMA fight, his first for Rings. I was in his corner when he took on Russian Mikhail Ilyukhin. This time, it was Randy who was on the end of some bullshit. Since Rings didn't use a cage, in the first round, the ref stood Randy and

Mikhail up when they were on the edge of the ring to move them to the middle. Randy was on top, and Mikhail was working for a kimura submission (a keylock hold where you take your opponent's arm and move it up their back, which fucks up the arm if there's no tap). Randy wasn't in too much trouble, he was in a good position to defend the attack if the ref had left them where they were. When they got repositioned in the center, Mikhail started cranking Randy's arm before the ref restarted the fight. It was a bush-league move, so when the ref yelled, "Fight," it was too late. Randy was forced to tap or risk getting his arm fucked up. He complained to the ref that Mikhail had cheated, but the ref didn't say shit. I was pissed and complained to the promoter who was watching from the side, but they wouldn't overturn it. The taste of fuckery once again.

Seven months later it was my turn. My contract was to fight in the Rings: King of Kings 1999 Tournament, a thirty-two-man open-weight-class tournament. After being around MMA for a couple years, the weight disadvantages didn't bother me anymore. I thought I could beat anyone. I saw that most of the time, the bigger guys were much slower and not as skilled as the smaller guys.

Rings guaranteed me $7,000 to show up and much more to win each fight and advance in the tournament. If by some chance I made it to the finals, which I didn't think I'd be able to do, my pay would be $30,000. I had never seen that type of money in the twenty-nine years I had been alive, but there was more. The promoters told me there would be a $200,000 bonus if I won the whole thing. At a press conference I was asked what I would do with the prize money if I won the tournament. I said, "I'm going to Disneyland Tokyo." *That would take a miracle*, I thought. I would have to win five fights in a row to do that, and I was only 4–0 in my young MMA career.

My first fight was against Bakouri Gogitidze, a former Olympic wrestler from the country of Georgia. Bakouri weighed a little more than 235 pounds, and I was going to get my first taste of fighting someone much larger than me right away. Randy and I had been sparring consistently, so I started to have a little more confidence in my punches landing. I knew I had power, I just didn't have placement.

I wanted to test out my striking with the larger Bakouri, but we went to the ground several times after he felt my punching power. I could tell he didn't like being hit. Believe it or not, there are some guys that don't like that feeling of bone on face, or thudding blows to the body. He was one of those. I had him in a front headlock and could hear Randy yelling, "Knee, knee, knee," and I started throwing some hard, cutting knees. *Fweeump! Ooooooo.* I landed a knee to his midsection and could hear the wind and fight taken out of Bakouri. His ass dropped like a sack of potatoes.

I was going to jump on top of him and planned on finishing the fight, but the ref stopped the fight. "Finished, finished, finished!" I guess Bakouri had tapped the canvas before I had a chance to do more damage on the ground. This guy was a silver-medalist wrestler in the Worlds but was the biggest pussy I had fought. And that goes for my whole career. He flat-out quit.

An hour later, my next fight was against Hiromitsu Kanehara, who had beaten Jeremy Horn in his first fight. Hiromitsu was a tough dude. He went out there and we brawled a bit. I got a yellow card for accidentally punching him while his face was down, but I had been able to do that in the UFC. Different promotions, different rules. I was able to control him for most of the fight by taking him down. I was awarded the victory after two rounds, albeit with some controversy. Rings rules stated that if the judges had it even after two rounds, there would be a third round. I'm not sure if the judges screwed up or not, because later I heard them say there should've been one more round. But it was too late. I would be moving forward in the tournament and fighting four months later, after the New Year.

I brought in the new millennium by accelerating my wrestling training for the 2000 Sydney Games with Randy and other Olympic-caliber wrestlers. In between sessions, I was preparing for my February 2000 fight (or fights if I moved on) in Japan. I still didn't think I was going to win the Rings tournament, but I was going to try.

The first fight was a quarterfinal match against Gilbert Yvel at the Nippon Budokan in Tokyo. This arena was bigger than the previous venue, and ironically, the Nippon was originally built to host judo competition in the 1964 Summer Olympics. That night, it was just a place to use my fighting skills to keep my Olympic gold-medal dreams alive.

Gilbert was a standup fighter, a good kickboxer, and already had twenty-three professional fights going into his match with me. I knew he had some dirty antics as well. In 1998 he had been disqualified for biting his opponent, and he was known to have a temper. In wrestling, if you're angry during a match, it will most likely work against you, so I wasn't worried about Gilbert's attitude.

DING, DING, the bell rang and I faked a takedown then threw a right hand that caught him flush in the face. He fell down but popped right back up. Before he had a chance to react, I immediately took him down for about ten to twenty seconds until we get stood up by the ref. That's when the dirty antics started. I took him down again and attempted an armbar, which he tapped to, but the ref let the fight keep going, and he was able to use his twenty-pound weight advantage over me by rolling out of the submission. *Okay, Dan, just keep working.* I put Gilbert in a north-south choke, and I was close to finishing it, when the dumb ref stands us up. *Like what the fuck?* He had no understanding that I was seconds away from turning Gilbert's lights out unless he tapped.

The rest of the fight was dirty bullshit fighting. Gilbert punched me in the back of the head, elbowed my spine, and grabbed the ropes. I was worn out after I had taken him down about fifteen times in ten minutes, but then had to hear him bitch and complain about it after. I thought, *Maybe you should've learned how to defend a takedown.* But that's the way guys were back then. Most of them weren't well-rounded fighters. I certainly wasn't, but I had to put myself in danger by fighting in their style too.

In the semifinals I faced future UFC Hall of Famer and future UFC and Pride Heavyweight Champion Antônio Rodrigo "Minotauro" Nogueira, known today as "Big Nog." He was much bigger than me, with a four-inch height and fifty-pound weight advantage. And he had phenomenal submissions. I don't know of anyone else my size that faced him. Those physical advantages of a bigger guy are the reason most people fight in their weight class.

Imagine a bantamweight (135-pounder) fighting a middle-weight who weighs 185 pounds. The 135-pounder would get demolished. It wouldn't be close. Hell, I looked to be every bit smaller than Big Nog.

I saw things a little differently. Why not test myself against the biggest, baddest, and best fighters out there? But I bit off a lot in Big Nog. He was a Brazilian jiu-jitsu black belt with years of boxing experience. When Big Nog was ten, he got run over by a truck and lost one of his ribs and part of his liver. Dude almost died. I knew he was no Bakouri. There would be no quit in Big Nog.

When the fight started, I found him to be extremely strong and good at latching onto me to get me down on the ground. I was able to scramble and get position on him, but someone with that size and decades of training was tough as fuck. In one of our early clinches, he was again trying to get me to the ground and jumped up to pull me down on him. I felt Big Nog's weight and ass land on my knee as we were falling. I heard my knee, *Pop! Fuck. That shit hurt.* I knew it wasn't good and could feel it was wobbly and super loose. I fought through it for two rounds, but the judges decided we needed to go one more round.

I wasn't happy but managed to get through another five minutes with Big Nog on my fucked-up knee. It felt like a thousand piranhas had sunk their teeth into it, then went to town on it. When the announcer was ready to declare the winner, I wanted to hear my name, but knew I had an uphill battle with my hurt knee.

"And the winner is—Dan Henderson!"

Wow. I did what I wasn't sure I could do. I made it to the finals. Every fiber, muscle tissue, ligament, and bone in my body, was just done. I was like a bucket of shit. My body felt worthless and unable to go one more fight. When I went to the locker room, the Rings officials came in and told me I had twenty minutes until the finals. I didn't say much, but my body language must've given something off. I could hear my cornermen, Randy and Ryan Parsons, talking in the background. I wasn't sure what they were saying, but it didn't sound like they had confidence that I would make it to the final fight.

Yep. Everyone can see I'm done. But what if I can win just one more? I knew I was guaranteed a $30,000 fight purse for the five fights over the two nights. That would help me pay some bills and not worry about finances going into the Olympic Trials. But I could sure use $200,000. It was life-changing money for me at that point. They might as well have said it was a million dollars.

My girlfriend, and future wife (now ex-wife), had just given birth to our one-year-old daughter. The fight money would undoubtedly be helpful, but the bonus money could help me with my new family. I needed to suck it up. *Dan, one more fight. Get up, and go handle business. Forget the knee pain. Just put a band-aid on it.* I could hear my dad in my head. What did I have to lose?

Before the finals started, they played the instrumental version of the American National Anthem. I didn't know they were going to do that, but I was singing the words in my head. Hearing that gave me goosebumps and motivated my ass to want to get up and go kick some ass. They played the Brazilian Anthem as well, but I was ready to represent for the United States. I still dreamt of a day when I would hear the National Anthem playing after winning a gold medal at the Olympics, but that could wait. I had $200,000 on the line.

Renato "Babalu" Sobral was my final test. I had reached the boss in a video game. I was like little Mario at the start of the tourney and morphed into Super Mario by making these finals to fight giant Bowser and save the princess. Except this wasn't a game. Babalu was coming to win. He was undefeated with twelve wins and ten victories being via knockout, TKO, or submission. He was another black belt in BJJ who would become the Strikeforce Light Heavyweight Champion of the world, and another larger guy who outweighed me by forty pounds.

DING, DING! We went forward like two battle rams and traded blows right away. I wanted to finish him quickly so I could rest my knee. But this motherfucker wasn't about to let that happen. After I was able to take him down, he illegally punched me a couple times in the back of the head, so the ref stood us up. My knee felt like Jell-O, but I was determined to leave everything I had out there. I threw a shitload of *Street Fighter II* uppercuts and punches that Babalu ate. I could tell the punches connected because he tried to tie me up every time I landed to his face.

After the first round was over, I know I did more damage and was the busier fighter. The next round was similar to the first. When I grabbed him with my left hand, I threw more power shots, and when he tried to take me down, I beat him to it. I was able to control him, and I threw punches to his body per Rings rules, which prohibited strikes to a downed opponent's face.

DING, DING, DING! The ref yelled, "Stop!" I looked over to the judges. They were tallying up their scores, and it seemed as if they had a winner. There wouldn't be a need for a third round.

I heard the announcer speak some Japanese and finally shouted, "Dan Henderson!" I couldn't believe I did it. Ryan lifted me up, and then I shook hands with Babalu and his corner. I walked back to the locker room with Randy and Ryan to get medically checked out before the Rings officials had me go back out for the champion ceremony.

The crowd showed their appreciation with applause, and I bowed to each side of the audience before stepping up on a platform they had put in the ring to recognize me as the winner. It wasn't the podium of my dreams, but it was still fuckin' cool. And the Rings promoters showered me with a ton of trophies, medals, and ribbons. They gave me so much shit, it took me a few years to get all of it back to the United States.

I felt it was well earned for giving everything I had for thirty-five minutes against a kickboxer; a boxer and BJJ specialist; and another striker and BJJ specialist. My body felt like it had been in a blender and rattled around for an hour. I was going home with my banged-up knee, but fuck, it was worth it. I'll never forget that day either, because February 26, 2000, was the *toughest* night of fighting I ever had in my twenty-year career. It's crazy to think that fighting more than once in one night was even a thing. Today, most fighters have no idea what it's like to fight two or three people in a day, but it was a real thing and can make for a short career for some who aren't able to handle that.

"Mister Henderson, would you like to check in that bag?" the ticket attendant joyfully asked as I was boarding the plane back to the States.

"No, thank you, I'm good."

I wasn't about to let this bag out of my sight or leave my hand. If someone at the airport happened to grab it, I knew they wouldn't get far. I wasn't going to lose all that money; even with my fucked-up knee, I would've chased them down and beat their ass. Simple. But I sure as hell wasn't going to be checking it in.

When the plane touched down on American soil, I was a little wary. The flight was long, but now I had to get this bag to my car and then home. We landed in Portland, Oregon, where I had moved with my wife-to-be and daughter just a few months before. Me and Randy had started Performance Quest, a gym where we could train wrestling and mixed martial arts. We were looking for like-minded individuals, and this is where we got the fight team name Team Quest—our first fight business venture. In addition to me and Randy, a future UFC star would come from our gym. He was one of the best shit talkers in MMA, but to us, he was just Chael Sonnen, the guy working at our front desk who trained wrestling and MMA alongside us.

Be cool, Dan. Nobody's worried about your stuffed bag. Did they really just hand me this bag? I had a flashback to winning the tournament. After I had won, I went to a banquet room the promoters had set up in the arena. They brought me a big, plastic Disney bag that looked like it had stuffed animals inside. *Whoompf,* they dropped the bag on a table in front of me. "It's all there, Dan." *Like, what's all there? A fuckin' dead body?*

I slowly opened the bag, half expecting a jack-in-the-box to fuckin' pop out at me. But nothing popped out. Inside was cold, hard cash, the most money I'd ever seen in my life. I didn't know there was that much printed money in the world. "Holy shit! I don't want this right now!" I blurted to myself and the Rings officials. I wasn't expecting this. A money order, check, or a wire was how I thought they were going to pay me. Instead, they had thrown $230,000 in American dollars in the bag, and now they wanted me to take off with it. *I don't think so.* I told them to give it to me when I get to the hotel, that way I can put it in the hotel safe. I didn't care how safe Japan was, I wasn't going to be taking a taxi with that much cash in a foreign land.

I made it safely to my car from the airport terminal and headed home with the prize money. I've never been flashy or needed nice, expensive jewelry, watches, or sports cars to fulfill me. Competing at the highest level did that for me. I've always tended to be practical. That's just what my parents taught me. Instead, I used some of the money to buy a new Ford Expedition, since I had a family of three and didn't want my newborn to be in a beater car. The rest I would save and use for rent, food, and other living expenses. I'm a pretty simple man. But I did appreciate how the Japanese paid their fighters. I didn't have to chase the promoter down or wait like I had to do in Brazil for my money. They always made sure to pay us right after the fights. And it was always in American money.

Fweet! The sound of the whistle starting or stopping action for a wrestling match. I had just finished wrestling in the 2000 Greco-Roman Nationals and looked at the scorer's table to see if I had won. *Shit. I lost.* I lost in the semi-finals and was going to have to wrestle in the Olympic Trials mini tournament once again. *I can never fuckin' catch a break!* Even though I had been the top guy for the past two Olympics, I still had to go through the fuckin' gauntlet like I was a rookie. If I had won nationals, I would've only had to wrestle against one guy to make the Olympic team.

I flew to Cali, Colombia, the following month for the 2000 Pan American Championships. It had no bearing on my Olympic status, but it was another test before the Olympics against the best wrestlers from countries in the Western Hemisphere. The Cuban I wanted to wrestle in 1998, Luis Méndez, would be at the Pan Ams again, and I was excited to test my mettle against him. He had already made the Cuban Olympic team, and we would see who would be the favorite from the Western Sphere.

It had been three months since I had torn my MCL, but I felt it was good enough to wrestle on. It wasn't 100 percent at the nationals tournament, but at the Pan Ams, it helped me get to the finals and face Luis. Those that were watching didn't think I had a chance to win; after all, I was the underdog, but I ended up beating him 3–2 to win gold. I was happy to have beaten one of the best guys in the world and was having a good year other than my knee and the nationals tournament hiccup.

When I got back to America, I was only home for a few weeks until the Olympic Trials started. I was the incumbent Olympian for that weight class, yet here I was trying to win a spot on the team for the third time. The shit went horrible. I lost my first match, and since it was single elimination, my 2000 Olympic dreams were gone within minutes. I waited four years of my life for less than ten minutes of wrestling. I was devastated. I was a much better wrestler than I had been in Atlanta, and I fuckin' lost before getting a real chance. I had let myself down, my country, Dad and Bob.

Instead, USA Wrestling was going to send me to the Olympics to be a training partner for the guys that made the team. I wasn't happy to be a backup, but I was happy to help out my fellow Americans at the 2000 Sydney Olympics. It was hard going there knowing I wouldn't be competing, but I knew the importance of that role as a training partner. Maybe it wouldn't have been so bad if I didn't have to watch the guy in my weight class, Quincey Clark, just shit the bed. He wasn't just terrible, but the worst.

If you're going to represent the United States, don't be scared and go there with zero confidence. Quincey didn't score *one* point. Not one. He lost 0–5 to the guy I had beaten a few months before, Luis Méndez, and got teched by the Egyptian wrestler 0–12. Done. Finished. I had fought and trained for four fuckin' years and had to watch this dude wear the red, white, and blue, wrestle like a high schooler, and come in *last* place. Fuck, it was painful and agonizing. Luis ended up coming in fifth (he beat the Egyptian) and the Egyptian eighth. I don't know if I would've medaled in Sydney, but I wasn't going to let these guys blow me the fuck out.

Quincey never went back to the Olympics. And in September 2022, he was arrested and charged with crimes against minors. He's innocent until proven guilty, but he's guilty of at least one thing—not showing up in Sydney.

★ ★ ☆

8

BACKSTABBER! | PRIDE: THE AXE MURDERER AND GRACIE KO

*T*ick, *Tick, Tick,* is the internal clock in all of us that tells us if we should stay in a room, a job, relationship, situation, or get the fuck out. You may not listen to that clock, but that doesn't mean your clock is wrong.

Following the Olympics, I knew I was going to have to make some choices about my career path. I was thirty years old and would have to wait another four years if I wanted to make the 2004 Athens Olympics. I thought I could still get better and improve my wrestling skills, but that didn't guarantee me an Olympic medal. Only one thing is certain in Olympic-level wrestling: nothing is certain.

My body *was* beat the fuck up from the wrestling grind; I had been wrestling twenty-five straight years of my life without any real break. I had added fighting in there, but like my dad, I had a family I needed to support. I wasn't going to make any money from the Olympic Committee, I wasn't the number-one guy in my weight class in America, and wrestling wasn't paying the bills anymore. Who the fuck am I kidding, they never really paid the bills anyways.

I stayed in Australia after the Olympics to visit a friend since I planned on heading straight to Japan to corner for Randy. Randy had also come up a little short and hadn't made the 2000 Olympic team (but was a semifinalist), and he was entering the new Rings: King of Kings Tournament. While I was in Australia, I contemplated all the decisions that were on the table for me.

Stick with wrestling; don't stick with it. Go back to chiropractic school; don't go back to school. Fight one more year, then call it quits. I didn't want to make a rash decision, but my body didn't feel like the well-oiled machine it had been before. Wrestling had taken a toll on my body, and I wasn't sure if four more years of wrestling would get me anywhere.

When I made my way to Japan, I came to somewhat of a decision with myself. I was no longer saying *fuck school*, but I wasn't in love with the idea either, so I would fight for one more year to make some money, and then go back to school. If my body still felt battered and worn out, I would quit competing.

I knew I liked the money, but how long would it last? I wasn't that old, but already, I started to feel like an aging stripper whenever I got an offer to fight. Every time I got paid, I started liking the cash even more. And, I started to fall in love with MMA. I had my buddy Randy to do it with, and MMA and wrestling were pretty similar.

Wrestling had a lot more repetitive elements to it, and I had mastered the moves, but I had a ton of shit to learn in MMA. They're both combative-type sports, but MMA was much more fun due to the multiple variables needed along with the technique, strength, and conditioning. Like wrestling, it's a one-to-one sport with a different ruleset, but I found myself drawn to it more and more.

I talked to my dad and Bob about fighting full-time, and they both supported it. Their blessing was all I needed. It was bittersweet, but I began to set new goals in mixed martial arts. Even though it hurt, I accepted the reality that my ultimate childhood dream didn't come true. I had to come to grips with the fact that I would never hear the National Anthem playing while standing atop the highest podium with an Olympic gold medal around my neck. But I was okay with it. I could shift my energy to my new love.

KNOCK, KNOCK. I went to the door, and there was the mailman standing with pen and paper in hand.

"Can you please sign this?" he asked.

"Why do I need to sign it?" I asked confused. I had never had to sign something from the mailman before.

"It's certified, sir. You're being subpoenaed for court."

When I opened the envelope, I glanced over the letter. *What the fuck? What a piece of shit.* I thought Rico had let me out of the contract. I hadn't heard from him after that. I guess he found out about my winnings at Rings and was claiming his company, which included him and his brother, was owed 20 percent. *Those greedy fucks.*

The first time I went to court, shit did not go well. I showed the judge a signed agreement between myself, Rico, and his brother Lou (who was president of RAW Promotions), which proved they had let me out of my contract. That judge didn't give a fuck. He wouldn't recognize it and said I owed them the 20 percent. I appealed the decision, and I was going to be irate if I had to fork over $23,000 to them for not doing shit. I wasn't going to settle with those crooks, and it was a good thing that I appealed. Due to the laws in California, which are friendly towards artists, entertainers, and apparently athletes and fighters—the new judge said the original contract was basically bullshit. The judge went on to say that Rico and Lou didn't have the authority to sue me because they weren't registered as an agent or manager with the State of California.

But why should they have gotten a penny anyways? They didn't negotiate it or do a damn thing for me. After that I had zero respect for them. I thought they were pieces of shit, and when I confronted Rico about it, he blamed it all on Lou. "Dan, this was all just a big misunderstanding. You know how my brother is."

Bullshit. Rico could've made it right and chose not to, so I didn't believe a word he said. What it came down to was that they had no integrity. They found out how much I made and tried to capitalize after the fact. Randy left them soon after the whole debacle as well. The good thing was, I was still able to take a life lesson from it. It's always been in my nature to learn from every situation, positive or negative. The lesson this time? Life is too short to have those types of people in your life.

My notoriety in mixed martial arts started to grow after the Rings tournament. It opened a door for me with another Japanese promotion, Pride Fighting Championships. They offered me the best fight contract I had seen to date. I wouldn't have to fight multiple assassins in one night either. The pay would be about $35,000 for my first fight, then it doubled for the second fight, with another increase for the third. I had never been paid that much for a single fight, let alone the exponential pay increases, so I agreed to the deal.

After I signed with them, they wasted no time in getting me a fight. They scheduled it two days before Christmas. No longer was I a wrestler who fought—I was officially now a fighter who was a pretty damn good wrestler. But I would soon find out I had magical powers in my right hand that would make my Olympic-caliber wrestling secondary.

Before I made my Pride debut, I went back to Japan to corner Randy in Rings, where he won his first two fights. After his wins, we headed back to the States, Atlantic City, New Jersey, where he took a fight in the UFC about a month later. He fought UFC Heavyweight Champion Kevin Randleman for a chance at the belt. Randy was able to TKO Kevin in the third round to become a two-time UFC champion. I lifted him up in the air just like he did for me after my wins.

I wasn't sure what was happening, but it felt like me and Randy's MMA careers were slowly starting to take off. We didn't know where it was headed, but our championship mindsets had us training in mixed martial arts more and more, day by day, and getting better each time. Before, we were just wrestlers trying to use our strengths to win fights. But our punching became crisper, kicks were more calculated, and our jiu-jitsu became smoother. We weren't the best at every element, but we were trying to be. We still had a long ways to go. Randy and I had bonded; we were like a band of brothers, helping each other every step of the way. He helped me, then I would help him. It was my turn to fight my first opponent in Pride when plans changed.

Three weeks before I headed to Japan, I went to Nice, France, which is thirty minutes from Monaco, for an international wrestling tournament. It was cool to go there because it gave me an opportunity to keep refining my wrestling skills, and there was no pressure to win.

While I was there, I came down with a sore throat, and was trying to gargle with salt and hot water to get rid of it, but it got worse. I went to the doctor, and just my luck, I had strep throat. My conditioning was fine right before I got sick, but now my body was in *get-over-this-sickness* mode. I went to the doctor and was given some antibiotics that didn't help my body heal any quicker.

But I wasn't going to call off the fight. How else would I get some cool Christmas gifts for my family?

Right before I was set to leave France, I received an email from my Japanese manager friend which read, "Hey, Dan, the fight with Vitor is off."

My first fight in Pride was supposed to be against the same guy Randy had beaten three years earlier, Vitor Belfort. Vitor was another guy who was outside of my natural weight class, but I had signed the fight agreement and was okay with the matchup.

"What? Why?" I replied back.

"He's hurt," he wrote. "Pride wants you to fight Wanderlei Silva."

I had never heard the name. "Who?"

"Wanderlei Silva. The Axe Murderer."

The Axe Murderer. Hmmmm. Whatever. I didn't care who I was fighting, just as long as I was fighting. I had mouths to feed. Even if it they wanted me to fight the Hulk or Arnold Schwarzenegger, I wouldn't have hesitated to say yes.

I arrived in Tokyo, Japan, a week before my fight. Usually, we would stay at the Tokyo Hilton, or an American-branded hotel. It was there I discovered the bidet. I had no idea what it was, all the buttons were in Japanese. But I soon learned when I pressed down on them, water would squirt up into my ass. It was a whole new experience, and I'd never leave Japan dirty.

I wasn't able to train at 100 percent, but pulling out of the fight was not an option. I called RAW wrestler and fighter Sean Bormet (who had fought Wanderlei three years before), to see what type of fighter Wanderlei was. I still didn't know what he looked like, but during fight week, while I was having breakfast, one of my corner guys pointed him out and said, "That's Wanderlei. The Axe Murderer. Nickname kinda fits, huh?"

I took a good look at Wanderlei to size up my competition. *Damn. This is who I'm fighting.* Shaved head? Check. Looks mean as fuck? Check. Tattoos on his head? Check. *Fuck. This guy does look kinda scary.*

I wasn't afraid of him, but he had the look of someone that wanted to kill somebody, that's for sure. Maybe if I hadn't seen guys that looked like him before, I might have been a little intimidated, but my whole life I had wrestled against guys that looked scary as fuck like Wanderlei. A lot of them turned out to be pussies. But then I would wrestle against guys that looked like harmless choir boys, and they would give me a tough time. That's why you never judge a book by its cover, or a person by their looks. After Wanderlei passed, I looked at some of my cornermen, and they were more taken aback than me.

December 23, 2000, was fight day. I was feeling a bit better, but I wanted to really impress the promotion and put on a good show. When we faced off in the middle of the ring, Wanderlei gave me his patented serial-killer gaze. "Oooooohhhhh. Ahhhhhhh." I could hear the 27,000 people in attendance murmuring when they saw Wanderlei staring me down. After watching his previous face-offs and fights, I saw his scary tactics had worked on other guys, but I found it amusing. I just smiled at him. There was no need to match his killer gaze. We'd be going at it seconds later.

Ding, ding! The fight got underway, and after I feinted a few times, we started swinging for the fences. *Plop!* I got dropped, and Wanderlei immediately jumped on top of me. He wasn't able to do much from that position except kick my legs and thighs. The ref stood us up and—*blam!* I did my patented level change and threw a right hand that dropped him to a knee for a second before he popped back up. I fuckin' cut him up pretty good. Blood started leaking from his eye, and, when we exchanged punches again, I sent him down again. He stumbled forward and instinctually grabbed me. Instead of making him stand with me, I went to the ground and started showering punches on him like he'd stolen something

from me. *Dammit*. It didn't finish him, and I started to feel the effects of my sickness creep back and my wind slowly seeping.

But Wanderlei's cut worsened. The blood leaked even more and looked like a sea of red ooze. That made the ref pause the action to let a doctor in the ring. They allowed him to keep fighting, but the shit got worse. Wanderlei's eye made him look like one of those big-ass aliens with those warty-looking heads from Star Trek. If this fight had been in the United States, it would've been over. But it wasn't. Wanderlei kept going, and we tussled until I ended up on the ground a little tired.

Fwoomp! He threw an illegal knee to the top of my head while my face was down. It was legal to throw knees or soccer kicks to someone with their face up, but mine wasn't. That rocked me a bit, and I grabbed my head thinking, *What the fuck?* He should've been at least deducted a point, and the move was grounds for disqualification, but it was never brought up. I had no plans on quitting anyways, but it was fucked up how the ringside doctors kept telling me I was okay, instead of asking me. But I learned some things were ass-backwards in Japan, and that was one of them. No dead body, no foul.

Towards the end of the round, Wanderlei was able to get the mount position, but then he stood up and tried to stomp my fuckin' head in, which was legal, but doing so while *illegally* holding on to the ropes. I'll fight by any ruleset, but holding on to the ropes to position a head stomp to generate greater force is some bullshit. Did the ref take any action? Nope. He just kept warning him.

By the second round I was done. My body hadn't fully recovered from strep, and I had nothing left, but was able to make it to the end. After twenty minutes of fighting, it went into the judges' hands, and they declared The Axe Murderer the winner.

Even though it was my first loss, I wasn't bitter, because although he was a tough fucker, I knew I could beat him, size difference and all. I knew his game. His whole persona is like one of those guys that needs to be mean and pump himself up to make his opponent the enemy (some guys are just like that), but in wrestling, you're wrestling against guys you know and may even be friends with. There was a mutual respect between us after that, but I wanted to fight his ass when I was at full strength. The fight also taught me to have confidence in my striking, and I should've kept the fight on its feet. My career from that point forward would be marked with standup wars and using my wrestling to avoid takedowns.

I've been underestimated since I was kid during wrestling tournaments when other kids or coaches would look at me. I wasn't a physical specimen, no strong beast like my brother, I just had to go out and prove my worth. After my opponents would face me, they would have a newfound respect for me, especially when I excelled. It seemed to be the same way in MMA. My competition learned I wouldn't back down.

When the New Year came in, I was able to finally fully recover from the strep throat. Pride reached out soon after and booked a fight between me and the legendary Renzo Gracie in March 2001. Even though I had lost to Wanderlei, Pride was still doubling my pay to $70,000 for the fight. That's the thing about Japan that I really liked. They didn't look at wins and losses like the UFC did (and still does to this day). They looked at how hard a fighter competes and the level of excitement brought to the fans. There's a lot of guys that win but are boring as fuck; then there are guys that lose but are exciting to watch. No matter the weight class, big or small, Japan rewarded those tough fighters and warriors getting in the ring.

Okay, Dan, let's not lose two fights in a row. I had watched tape on Renzo and saw he looked good on his feet because of his previous opponents, but his real strength was submissions on the ground. It was simple Gracie Jiu-Jitsu 101, and I had to be careful of armbars, triangle chokes, rear naked chokes, and kimuras. My game plan was to keep the fight standing. I didn't want to be defending a shitload of submissions and get caught, but I knew if he felt my power, he would try to take me down. For my fight with Renzo, I trained a little differently. I put on these big sixteen-ounce boxing gloves while training partners would wear the small four-ounce MMA gloves. My goal was to train with the big gloves so I could get my punches more accurate and defend any takedowns from those punches.

The training paid off. We shook hands before the start of the fight, and he came out and threw a kick. I countered with my right hand, and he immediately shot in for the takedown. I could tell he didn't want to stand with me. I defended the takedown with a sprawl, and he attempted a couple more takedowns that didn't work. I had the fight right where I wanted it. Face to face. I figured out his timing, and that's when Renzo dipped his head and threw a punch, but I countered with my new punch, later to be dubbed the "H-Bomb" by Pride commentator Mauro Ranallo, which instantly turned the light out of my opponents. Renzo shot in for a takedown and *wham!* The thundering right hand instantly crumpled Renzo. *Keep going, Dan, don't let him get back up.* I rotated my body to where his head fell and threw a left uppercut to his face because I wasn't sure he was out, then I saw his body go limp, and I immediately stopped my assault.

DING, DING, DING. The bell rang out, and the ref stopped the fight. I had just won my first Pride fight. When I watched the fight over and listened to the commentary, initially, they had no idea what had happened. They thought his head hit the mat and that's what knocked him out. It wasn't. I hit him so hard, my right knuckles were sore, and there were two little red dots where his jawbone met his neck from my knuckles leaving that imprint. I had never wrapped my hands before a fight, but after the KO, I wrapped them every fight after. I didn't want to fuck up my knuck-les on someone else's face.

After the ref waved off the fight, I looked and saw his brother, Ryan Gracie, who was known to be the crazy Gracie in the fam-ily who started shit with people, jump in the ring to tend to his brother. I didn't know if I was going to have to defend myself and fight him right there for knocking his brother out, but everything ended up being cool. Besides, I had a prime Randy Couture in my corner as usual, who was about to defend his UFC heavyweight title in just over a month.

It took a few minutes for Renzo to come to, but I shook his hand and gave him a little hug, and there was mutual respect between us. Even today, I've always respected him and what he's done for the sport as one of the pioneers along with Royce and Rickson. Those original Gracies were fuckin' tough. And they've turned a fuckload of black belts into good fighters. I'd already fought a handful of their fighters and would continue to do so in my career. And it was good to see the loyalty Ryan had for Renzo, so I was saddened when I heard about Ryan unfortunately dying in 2007 under some mysterious circumstances in a Brazilian jail.

☆☆☆

9

STEROIDS, MUCH? GO PISS IN A PAPER CUP

Which NFL team was the greatest of all time? The undefeated 1972 Miami Dolphins or the one-loss 1985 Chicago Bears? What about the 49ers and Cowboys of the '90s? Let's not forget Tom Brady and all the variations of Super Bowl teams he's been on.

Comparing the greatest NFL or NBA teams and eras is similar to the question I get questioned frequently today about the Pride versus UFC era. Who had the better fighters, which promotion was top dog, and why weren't you in the UFC at the time?

There's no question Pride had the superior fighters, because many would jump over from the UFC to get a better payday. I could've spent my entire career in the UFC, but up to that point, I wouldn't have been paid close to what I was getting in Pride. It didn't make sense financially. To give some context, the money Pride was paying guys back in the 2000s was more than what the UFC is paying a majority of their fighters today. We would have been fools to be exclusive for the UFC at that time. No one knew where the sport was going, and I needed to make the most money I could for my family.

My next fight in Pride was just about two months after my fight with Renzo. I wasn't hurt, so I told the promoters I was available to fight when they needed me, and they booked me right away. I was also coming up close to the one year I had given myself to reevaluate how my body felt after fighting. I had promised myself I would make a final decision—back to school or stick with fighting.

It didn't take long for me to think it out. Ironically, my body didn't feel worn out from fighting. I found that training mixed martial arts wasn't grinding on my body like wrestling was. Besides, I was about to be thirty-one years old and didn't think I could make the same money as a chiropractor right away.

I was booked to fight Japanese fighter Akira Shoji, which was the last fight on that contract. I knew how important final fights on your contract could be, so I wanted to make sure I performed well going into negotiations. The word was Akira was tough—warrior tough. Fellow American and MMA fighter Guy Mezger warned me about his only offensive strength, "Besides his durability, make sure you watch out for his overhand right. That's it."

Akira may have never become a champion, but he embodied the samurai spirit. Rumor had it that before every fight he would make sure his house was clean and in order, and he had an up-to-date will just in case he *died* in the ring. That seemed a bit intense to me. I knew the dangers of what I was signing up for, but I've always tried to have positive thoughts going into fights. Akira? He was willing to be killed—death before dishonor.

Craaaaack! A punch caught me. *Fuck, it was that damn overhand right Guy warned me about!* The reality was, I didn't see that punch coming. It was a perfectly timed shot, which put me on autopilot from there. I knew what was going on, but didn't have my full wits to drive manually, so I let the machine inside of me take over. The hours of sparring, thousands of hours of grappling, and numerous wrestling matches had put my skill on another level from Akira, so the machine in me just went forward. After that rocking punch, I started to piece him up with my punches and fight acumen. He really didn't have a chance.

Most of the guys I fought would've been done much sooner, but not Akira. On one exchange, I dropped him so bad that I stopped my barrage and signaled to the ref to stop the fuckin' fight. The ref wouldn't do it, so I hopped back on him and started whooping him up some more. I felt bad that the ref didn't stop the onslaught sooner. In the third round, they were going to need a gurney if the fight continued, and when the ref saw that, he finally put an end to the beatdown. The record books will show that I TKO'd Akira, but it won't reveal his fortitude in taking a beating and damage while never giving up.

When my contract ended, Pride was ready to re-sign me right away. They offered me $100,000 for my next fight, my first six-figure deal, and my pay was to go up once again after every fight. For mixed martial arts in 2001, that was more than fair to me. I was getting paid more in mixed martial arts than in all my years of wrestling combined. It was good to feel appreciated by the promotion, and I didn't have to let them know my worth. They already knew it.

Me and Randy were able to provide for our families with the money coming in. We didn't have to scrounge for sponsorships or seminars to pay rent. And, thankfully, I never had to take another cent from my dad. Even if my career had come to a halt, I had enough saved to last me until the next episode. Good thing there wouldn't be another episode for a while.

Murilo "Ninja" Rua was my fourth Pride fight. I didn't know it would be a foreshadowing of my infamous fights with his younger brother, Maurício "Shogun" Rua, in the future, but Ninja was a tough dude. I fought him at the Tokyo Dome in November 2001, in front of the biggest crowd I had ever competed for before. The Tokyo Dome was built as a baseball stadium but was also being used for concerts and other events as well. When I made the walk at that big-ass stadium, it was a complex experience. To get to the walkout area, I had to go up an elevator, down some stairs, through some doors, up another elevator, and finally to the walkout entrance. There was a sold-out massive audience of about fifty-five thousand people, almost triple the max capacity at the modern T-Mobile Arena in Las Vegas.

My fight with Ninja went all three rounds, and although he was another tough fighter, I thought I had done enough to win. He was well-rounded, and a couple times after I hurt him, I tried to shove him to the ground after punching him because I thought he might just collapse, as we both had gotten pretty winded. After the scorecards were read, I got my hand raised and was back on a three-fight win streak.

After the Ninja fight, I faced two more tough Brazilians. First up was Ricardo Arona, who was both super strong and super 'roided up. I wanted to stand and strike with him, but after I caught him with punches, he would just take me down and tried to hump me. He knew he wasn't going to finish me, so he played it safe by laying on top of me. I went on to lose by split decision, but what hurt more is that I would've gotten a rematch with Wanderlei, who was the Pride Middleweight Champion (middleweight was 205 pounds in Japan).

My fight with Arona was in April 2002, and I was waiting for a phone call hoping to get one more fight by the end of the year, but then on December 13, 2002, I heard from my Japanese contact. "Hey Dan, they want to see if you can fight Big Nog on December 23."

I had been training but wasn't expecting such a last-minute call. "That's in ten days."

"Yes. His opponent got hurt. Can you do it?"

Okay, they want me to fight Big Nog, who is now the Pride Heavyweight Champ. In ten days. "Yeah, I'll do it," I said.

I didn't like the idea of turning down fights. Even with no fight camp, I was still willing to get in there to take on Big Nog, whose only loss was to me. I wasn't out of shape, but I wasn't in shape to fight someone fifty pounds heavier than me either. Big Nog had won the Rings: King of Kings Tournament in 2000, and the year after won the Pride heavyweight belt. If that wasn't impressive enough, he had already defended the title four times, and rattled off twelve straight wins since we had faced off.

Our fight went back and forth for two rounds. He didn't want to stand and strike with me, and I didn't want to be on the ground with him. Big Nog had gotten stronger, and I was trying to survive his kimura, armbar, and plethora of other submission attacks. By the third round, I was pretty fuckin' tired. And the longer the fight went, the more the weight made a difference. Big Nog used every pound to his advantage. He wasn't trying to lose his belt or another fight to me. Big Nog was finally able to secure an armbar a few minutes before the fight was going to end, and he retained his title.

I sometimes think back to that fight and wonder, *What if?* Maybe instead of becoming a future two-weight champion, I would've been a three-weight champ. A feat that *no* fighter has done in any major MMA promotion. What made it worse was when the fight was over, the judges told me I was winning at the time of the armbar.

But you can't change the past. We never got a rubber match, but he's just one of those guys I matched up well against. I could beat Big Nog 100 percent of the time with a training camp because of our fighting styles. He can't take me down when I'm in peak condition, and I beat him standing as well. That's why styles make fights.

My fight with Big Nog was the last fight on my contract, and it was the first time in my career I had lost two straight fights. I thought it might affect my stock, but Pride didn't see it that way. Neither did the Japanese people. They saw me as entertaining as fuck, as a savant who was willing to fight anyone. In the streets of Japan, I got recognized quite a bit. After every fight, more and more people started to know who I was, because Pride was in the homes of millions of people watching on television. When I would get back to the States, there would be people here that recognized me who had bought the Pride pay-per-views, but my celebrity was also big in Europe.

In 2005, I was walking around in Paris when all of sudden some dude stopped his car in the middle of the street, swung the door open, hopped out, ran over to me, and said, "Dan Henderson!"

I gave him a half smile. "Yeah?"

I could tell he was surprised. But he just repeated himself, "Dan Henderson," and put his hand out to shake mine.

I guess that was the only English he knew, but it was a crazy scene. The dude left his car in the middle of the street with his door hanging wide open. I never got into wrestling or fighting to be famous, but from that point on, I became recognized more and more.

Pride events were gaining more traction with fans worldwide as well. The promotion's brand was rising, their sponsorship deals were skyrocketing, and they offered me a new contract with a bump in pay despite coming off *two* losses.

After I signed my new deal, I was curious about the size, strength, and massive muscles that some of the Pride fighters had. They didn't look natural to me. It didn't matter to me if they were doing some shit, but I was still curious about their doping tests. In wrestling, we had the World Anti-Doping Agency (WADA), who would test us year-round and at any time of the day. It could be 6:30 a.m. or 10:00 p.m. and those dudes would be knocking on my door. I was never worried; I had never tested positive my whole wrestling career, and they took their job seriously. The WADA representatives would watch me as I pissed in a cup, then they would personally grab it and seal it themselves. They would be so close to me pissing, the steam would be coming from it as I passed it to them.

"Don't burn yourself," I told one of them jokingly.

When I posed the question to the Pride official, his only response, half-jokingly, was, "If we tested everyone for steroids, we'd only have you and Nogueira fighting!"

I knew what he was trying to say. Most of those fuckers fighting were on some fuckin' wacked-out carrot-juice steroids. I'm sure that most of the guys I fought were on something as well. And what made things worse was this half-act like they would be testing. Before fights, a Pride organizer would hand me a paper cup and tell me to go use the bathroom and give it back to them whenever. No one followed me, nobody looked to see where or how I got the piss. You could easily pass it to someone else to piss for you. I'd do it myself and hand the paper cup back to them, unsealed. I probably could have put apple juice in there and they wouldn't have cared. Once I gave it to them, there was no record of it or trace of it again.

I tried to push for more intricate testing when I went back to the UFC as well. I told them WADA would be able to weed out the fighters who were abusing the system with the shit they were taking. I was outspoken on the topic and figured I would beat the cheating juiceheads at any rate. Still, it wasn't a level playing field.

Just look at some of the guys I fought in Pride. My first fight in, and there's a jacked-up Wanderlei who looked mean and meaty as fuck. And how'd he survive my onslaught and keep up with me with those big-ass muscles? Steroids. He admitted years later that he was taking banned substances. I didn't fight Alistair Overeem, but I remembered seeing him one year where he was lean and athletic, then twelve months later, the dude put on a hundred pounds of pure fucking muscle. That ain't normal. He also got busted years later, but it was obvious for the most part who was on them. But as years went by, some fighters got better at passing some of the tests. When I fought Vitor Belfort in Vegas, I beat his ass, and then he got popped for 4-hydroxytestosterone, a banned synthetic anabolic-androgenic steroid. I fought him twice after that, and it was obvious he was on something that made him even bulkier, but with those fights being in Brazil, he passed their Mickey Mouse test.

In 2015, the UFC finally brought in the United States Anti-Doping Agency (USADA), a signatory of WADA, but it came at the tail end of my career. They've done a good job catching some of these steroid users, but as long as athletes want an edge, they're always going to look for ways to game the system and get around it. That's just the way it is. There's much more money in winning than losing, and some of these fuckers need it to be mentally confident in themselves. Look at fuckin' baseball. They figured out how to put some cream on themselves to whack the shit out of the balls. Barry Bonds and Mark McGwire were doing things never done before. The difference between baseball, football, or any other sport is that they aren't getting inside of ring or cage to try and kill somebody. Fighters are constantly trying to shut another motherfucker's lights out. It could be temporarily or permanently. I wasn't going into a fight trying to kill somebody, but that's one of the risks of getting in there.

My next three fights I went on a first-round-knockout spree. In March 2003, I fought Shungo Oyama and threw my H-Bomb. It caught him in the chin and already had him knocked out, but I grabbed him, and he looked like a bobblehead as I drove him to the ground to add a few more punches to officially end the fight. It had been a year and a half since my last win, so I was happy as fuck afterwards to get back in the win column.

Eight months later I took on the Brazilian Murilo Bustamante, who was the former UFC Middleweight Champion. He never lost the belt, but decided to vacate it to sign with Pride for what was probably a shitload more money. He had been around for a while and fought the likes of future UFC Light Heavyweight Champion and Hall of Famer Chuck Liddell and future Pride and UFC Light Heavyweight Champion Quinton "Rampage" Jackson.

He had come up short against Rampage the fight before, losing by split decision, but I was able to take care of Murilo in less than a minute. In front of a record Pride crowd of almost seventy thousand people, I hurt him with a punch, then kneed him to the face and turned his lights out. I followed that up with a few more punches until the ref stopped the fight.

That is one fight I will always remember because of the sea of people in attendance. It was the largest crowd I fought in front of, more people than a Super Bowl usually has. The only attendance that was bigger in MMA was a co-promotion between Pride and K-1 where over ninety-one thousand people showed up. The crowds overseas were huge. Even today, the most packed arenas in America hold less than twenty thousand fans.

In 2004, I had another good year, which went almost the same way as 2003 did. I finished my first opponent, Kazuhiro Nakamura, in the first round when his shoulder dislocated, but I was already on the way to finishing him.

Fighting had become part of my DNA. First, it had been wrestling, but I was so enamored with the fight game, I wanted to beat everyone I came across. It was my martial arts of choice, knocking people senseless and wrestling, versus whatever the fuck my opponent wanted to do. I thought my weapons of choice were simply better than anyone else's. There's only one way to find out who is better. And, at thirty-three years old, I had goals of being a world champion. I didn't dwell on the past.

Pride then booked me to fight on their New Year's Eve card, Shockwave 2004, versus Yuki Kondo. You've probably never heard his name before, and a fighter of this caliber would usually be menial compared to the guys that I've fought, but this fight is one I will never forget fight 'til the day I die, because I felt absolutely horrible going into this fight, like I wanted to die.

Pride fights were usually on Sunday afternoons, so we'd leave the hotel around 10:00 a.m. to get to the arena. But fight day morning, I woke up at 2:00 a.m. and puked my guts out. The sushi, noodles, and grilled chicken I had eaten had made its way from my stomach into the hotel room toilet. Japanese food was usually really good, and I liked sushi and other food they had, but I was either poisoned or ate some bad shit.

I called the Pride officials and notified them I was not feeling good and was sick as fuck. I did not know how I was going to pull off a fight. When I got to the arena, they sent a doctor to the locker room where I had a fever of 103 degrees. My body couldn't handle any type of food, and taking a sip of water made me gag. I started to get dehydrated, and since I couldn't take in fluids, they gave me an IV with four bags of fluids. Then they sent in another doctor for a grand finale. The doctor, who had small hands, shoved some small pills up my ass so they could bring my fever down. They *really* wanted me to fight, and it was going to take more than a sickness for me to pull out of the fight. I attempted to warm up but couldn't even do that. I felt like I had the strength of a six-year-old. The Pride officials wouldn't have said anything if I didn't fight. They knew I looked like shit, but I decided to fight anyway.

I felt the fatigue as soon as the bell rang. I tried to quickly finish Yuki with a guillotine while I was mounted on top of him, but he was able to wiggle out. *Ah, shit. This is going to be a long fight.* The fight was fuckin' rough as shit. I got kneed in the stomach in the first round and almost puked, but there was no food in my stomach, and then I got hit with a yellow card for what they deemed as stalling. Even the commentator, Bas Rutten, a legend of the sport, said, "This doesn't look like the Dan Henderson we know."

I felt like dying. Death was beckoning for me to lay it down. And the fight went the full twenty minutes, where I narrowly won by split decision. Afterward, when I went to get paid, they tried to dock me 10 percent for the yellow card. Pride rules made it so fights were action packed, and when they weren't, fighters would be given yellow cards that would immediately be deducted from their purse. I wasn't having it. When they told me that, I knew we were going to have a problem.

"Fuck that. Pay me my full money," I said. "I didn't have to fight on this fuckin' card. I did it anyway. You're not going to take out any of the fuckin' money I fought for."

With that, they paid me my whole purse. I figured they were just trying to save as much money as they could, but I didn't have to go out there and lay it on the line for them. But I did, for better or worse. I didn't want war outside the ring, but I was always prepared for it.

10

LITTLE LEPRECHAUN WHO? | FIRST DOUBLE CHAMPION

In early 2005, Pride had only two championship belts, the heavy-weight and middleweight divisions. My eyes had been set on the middleweight champ, Wanderlei. And just when it seemed like I'd get my shot at the belt, I'd lose a fight that would take me out of the title picture. I could've taken the heavyweight belt off of Big Nog, but it seemed like the belt was always just out of my reach. It was like chasing a gold medal all over again. Close to the podium but never on it.

It didn't help when I fought for the first time in 2005. In April, I headed over the Pacific to face Antônio Rogério Nogueira, or, to most, "Little Nog," the twin brother of Big Nog. Unlike his larger brother, he fought at 205 pounds. On my way to Japan, I ended up getting a head cold, which moved into my chest, and the week of the fight I couldn't breathe very well. Still, early on in the first round, I was able to control the fight and was beating Little Nog's ass with my standup, but like his brother, he was durable and tough. As the fight continued, it became harder to breathe, and I got caught in an armbar after eight minutes of fighting. The loss broke my four-fight win streak, but worse, a rematch with Wanderlei was farther away.

The Pride officials knew I was fighting much bigger guys, so after the fight, they asked me if I wanted to fight at 185 pounds in their welterweight division. I told them it didn't matter to me. If they needed me to go down a weight class, it was closer to my natural wrestling weight division anyways.

They said they were putting together a Pride Welterweight Grand Prix and would be adding a championship belt to the division. *Well, if I can't get a fight with Wanderlei, at least I can win a belt at welterweight,* I thought to myself. The only caveat about the Grand Prix tournament was I would have to fight more than once in a night if I won. The belt was my goal, so if I needed to fight ten times in a night, I would've. And, on September 25, 2005, I fought multiple times because the only thing that could stop me from being a world champion was myself.

My first fight of the night was against Ryo Chonan, which didn't last long. I took one leg kick, then made quick work of him by knocking him out in just over twenty seconds. I had learned from my early UFC and Rings tournament days that I did not want long, grueling fights. The fresher a fighter is for their subsequent fights, the better.

The second fight, against Akihiro Gono, went a bit further into the first round. In the first couple minutes, we got tangled up going to the ground, and our heads accidentally collided. The ref stopped the action because of the headbutt, and when the action resumed, our heads grazed again. Akihiro complained to the ref that I had done it on purpose. I thought, *What the fuck?*

The ref stood me up and gave me a yellow card for that bullshit. I wanted to hurry up and beat his ass after that. He was another tough Japanese fighter, but guys that were my size stood no chance against my power. I finally caught him with my H-Bomb, which broke his jaw and sent him spiraling to the ground. I added a few more punches for good measure, but the ref came in and waved the fight off. I was headed to the finals!

The finals were set a few months later for Pride's New Year's Eve event on December 31, 2005. I'd face a familiar foe, Murilo Bustamante, who'd won his side of the Grand Prix bracket and was the Brazilian I knocked out silly in our fight two years before. I didn't expect this fight to the be the same; the quick knockout over Murilo didn't mean he was a pushover. He had put together three straight wins, finishing two of his opponents.

When I made the walkout for my first championship bout, I could feel the electricity in the crowd. The New Year's card had added production from Pride. It was a special event with fifty thousand roaring fans. We were the main event, and the Japanese people were there to see who would be crowned Pride Welterweight Champion of the World.

The championship fight felt like the Super Bowl. There would be no blowout. Murilo wanted the fight on the ground but was still willing to trade shots with me. He caught me with a good punch that cut me below my left eye, but that was the most damage he would do to me. I rocked him with my big right hand, which buckled him, then threw some knees to drop him to his back. I tried to finish him, but he wouldn't go away. He was one tough SOB. I've always been the type of fighter to say, "Fuck winning by points," but sometimes, there's no way around it. The fight went the distance, and the first judge thought Murilo won (I was shocked as hell when I heard that), then the second two judges scored the fight for me.

I heard the ring announcer scream, "Dan Heeeenderson," and it dawned on me that I had finally won the first championship belt in my career! I had reached one of my mixed martial arts goals. I could check "world champion" off of that list. After five years in Pride, I had the championship belt placed around my waist. The Japanese, always known to be ceremonious, put on this grand celebratory ceremony after the fight. I couldn't stop pinching myself. I was the best 185-pound fighter in the world.

After I became Pride champion, more people started to take notice. *Full Contact Fighter* magazine had been one of my sponsors early on, but more companies reached out and threw me a little bit of money to put their logo on my walkout shirts and trunks. There weren't any major brands like Reebok or Monster getting behind fighters, but the additional fanfare and autographs made me feel like I was doing something right. I felt like I was just getting my MMA career started at thirty-five and was determined to keep riding the train.

When I got back to California, I was congratulated by my friends and family. There was a handful of people that wanted a picture with the big, sturdily built, silver-plated belt Pride had designed. It felt good to finally be the best in the world at something, but when I got home, it was business as usual. I tended to my family and got right back to training. I felt like I was still chasing something in the MMA world. There was work to be done.

After settling in at home after the New Year, I got a call to fight in Pride Bushido 10. Bushido was still part of the Pride brand, but there were some variations to those events. They would use their Bushido cards to put different fight teams against each other or showcase up-and-coming fighters. To be honest, it was confusing as fuck, so I didn't ask questions, I just fought.

In April 2006, they put me up against Kazuo Misaki in a non-title fight. Why? I don't know. He was in my weight class, but Pride didn't put my title on the line for the fight. I beat Kazuo by unanimous decision, but then they wanted me to fight him four months later. I questioned one of the Pride officials, "What the

fuck? I just beat him. Why do you want me to fight him again?"
I never got a clear answer; they didn't seem to care. They wanted
me to fight him on another Bushido card and make it part of the
Pride 2006 Welterweight Grand Prix. I told them that shit made
less sense. Why would I fight in a welterweight grand prix when I
was champ? And my title wouldn't be on the line again. I was frus-
trated by the situation and unmotivated to fight Kazuo.

On fight night, I was lackadaisical and had a tough time getting excited for the rematch. I came out flat, just going through
the motions. I wasn't sick, I wasn't out of shape, there was nothing
wrong with me, but I lost a decision. My four-fight win streak had
been broken.

When you go to war, one shouldn't be complacent or lax, even
when they've defeated an enemy already. I understood that, but
in war, an enemy doesn't come back to life either. I wanted a new
challenge—and I got that when Pride rang my line.

"Hello, Dan?"

"Yep," I said.

"Do you want to fight Vitor in October," they asked.

Vitor was a fight I couldn't take lightly, so I was motivated
to finally be able to fight him. It was on short notice, and on top
of that, Pride asked me to go up in weight and fight him at 205
pounds. I didn't ask any questions; I wanted to bounce back from
my lackluster performance against Kazuo.

The fight was also to take place on American soil for the first
time in Pride history, so it made sense to put one of their biggest
American stars on the card. They also knew I was proud of my
country, a former US Olympian, and with Pride looking to tap
into the US market, I would be able to fill some seats in the Las
Vegas venue, two and a half hours away from my hometown.

Pride had a monopoly overseas as the biggest mixed martial
arts promotion in the world, but the UFC was beginning to rival

them. At first, it was a friendly competition; Pride and the UFC had even exchanged fighters a couple times, but only the hardcore fans in America knew who the superstars of Pride were: Fedor Emelianenko, Big Nog, Mirko Cro Cop, Wanderlei, Shogun, Mark Hunt, and a handful of others. Pride wanted to expand their brand with the growing American audience.

On October 21, 2006, Pride showed off their brand to American fans, and it was my first time fighting in the States in over eight years. I was a much different fighter from my last outing in America, and I wanted to make new memories. Besides, I had my displaced jaw and memories from the hospital to always remember my fights in Mobile.

When I walked, I noticed there wasn't close to the number of people in attendance that we'd had Japan, but I had also forgotten how different an American audience is. Even though there were less than fifteen thousand people, I could hear the cheers and jeers from the crowd. There wasn't a crowd better than the other, but I had gotten used to the huge crowds in Japan being relatively quiet during fights. They also understood the techniques and moves more than the American audience, especially grappling. American crowds have caught up in their fight knowledge of submissions and techniques, but they still have a preference for huge knockouts, whether it be by punch or kick. The American audiences will also boo grappling when they feel it's going on too long. Once the blood starts flowing, be it squirting from someone's eye, or a nose leaking with snot and cartilage flying out—you'd think we were in a Roman coliseum back in the gladiator days. In Japan, the fans rarely booed. Big punches, submission attempts, and throws elicited *oooos* and *ahhhhhs* from them; they applauded every fighter; and they rooted for the smaller guy to win because their guys were often the smallest in MMA. Their quiet respectful nature seemed to be a part of their culture. The juxtaposition between the two was clear. If you blindfolded me and put me in the middle of an American and then a Japanese arena, I could tell you what country I was in based off the crowd noise.

The fight with Vitor played out close to what I had thought. We had mutual respect for each other, and he knew my team pretty well. He had fought Randy, and we had been on the same fight cards before. I felt like I needed to take him down in the first round to mitigate his explosive power, and my plan was to break him mentally and physically while he was down on the mat. I saw myself finishing him in the third round, either by knocking him out on his feet or by beating the fuck out of him on the ground. I told my corner to remind me of my plan to finish him in the third round, but it must've slipped their minds.

For the most part, the fight proceeded in this way. I took Vitor down, but at certain points, stood up with him and exchanged strikes. I tried to impose my will on him and wear him out, but he was one of the toughest fighters out there, and there was no clear opening for me to finish him. The fight went the distance, and I won a unanimous decision with one judge scoring the bout 30–24 in my favor.

I was happy to get a win in my home country, and I earned a career-high $250,000, which left me with two fights on my contract. It seemed like I would never leave Pride. They treated me right, and I was guessing that my next fight would be a defense of my title in Japan close to the New Year, but when December came around, there still wasn't a call.

My win against Vitor helped my stock rise with fans, so I thought Pride was trying to figure out who would be the biggest fight for me at welterweight. But when they reached out to me in January 2007, I was surprised by what they had planned.

"Dan, are you available to fight next month?" one of the Pride officials asked.

I don't know why they ever asked if I was available, of course it was going to be a yes. They should've just told me what they were going to ask.

"We want you to fight Wanderlei in Vegas in February, if that's okay?"

I wanted to say, "What took so long?" I'd finally be able to avenge my first loss in MMA, which still bothered me.

I knew I could beat anyone I had lost to, but Wanderlei had gone on a middleweight run like no other, and I didn't think they would give me another chance at him. He had held on to the belt for six years, a phenomenal feat. During his string of wins, he had beaten the "Gracie Killer" Kazushi Sakuraba twice, knocked out future UFC Light Heavyweight Champion Quinton "Rampage" Jackson twice, and beaten fellow juicer Ricardo Arona. I was about to face the best version of Wanderlei Silva, who was in his prime, for his middleweight belt. I had a chance to be a current two-weight champion. That shit gave me tingles. It was for all the marbles. I wouldn't have had it any other way.

February 24, 2007, was the date of my redemption. I had pushed myself harder than I ever had during training and didn't want to let the fight slip through my hands. If I lost, it wouldn't have been for a lack of grit or determination. When going to war, if you don't figure out what you did wrong the first time, maybe you're not the right soldier or general for the job.

"You ready? You ready? You ready? *Gooo!*"

The referee let us loose, and we started with a quick touch of gloves. I had done research and watched Wanderlei's fights at 205 pounds and saw why people thought he was practically untouchable. He also had new bulging muscles that hadn't been there in his first fight. It looked like his muscles had muscles, which gave off a scarier aesthetic. For good measure, he added more tattoos in addition to the tattoo on the back of his head, which gave his Axe Murderer moniker a nice polish too. The motherfucker definitely looked and played the part.

There would be no feeling-out process. I started by throwing an inside leg kick, and a few seconds later we started trading big bombs. *Craaack.* I caught him with a huge shot and the fight was on. I slipped during the exchange, and Wanderlei capitalized by jumping on me. I was able to defend pretty well, so he wasn't able to do much. I could hear the ref yelling, "Action! Action!"

There were whistles and chants from the crowd to stand us up, and the ref finally obliged and put us back on our feet. We exchanged more punches, and the crowd started to chant, "Silva, Silva, Silva!" It didn't bother me that they were rooting for a Brazilian. All that mattered was that they were into the fight. Towards the end of the first round, I started to feel my right hand throbbing. I tried to throw my left hook more to avoid the pain in my right hand, but when Wanderlei came near me, I unleashed my right, trying to win by any means necessary.

DING, DING, we headed to our corners, and I shook my head and told my cornermen, "My fuckin' right hand is hurting." I heard nothing but crickets. In fact, they didn't even look at my hand or acknowledge what the fuck I'd said.

"Dan, you know what to do. Keep your hands up and let your left hand set up the big right." *They are really not addressing my hand. So maybe I shouldn't either.* I figured if they're not going to talk about it, I won't worry about it. *Put a fuckin' band-aid on it.*

DING, DING, the fight resumed. I wanted a knockout, he wanted a knockout, and the crowd just wanted someone to get knocked the fuck out. In the second round, I opened up a cut by his right eye, and took him down to soften him up with strikes. I could tell he knew I was starting to get the edge on him.

When the final round started, Wanderlei looked like a fresh fighter. I had flashbacks of our first match and him cruising to victory in the third round. He wanted me out of there and threw power punches trying to knock my head off. I was able to land a strike of my own, a spinning backfist that landed square on his chin. The shot stunned him but didn't put him in any danger.

The round continued and I thought maybe the fight would go to a decision again. Wanderlei didn't want to leave the crowd without a knockout—we were the main event, after all—and he started to wind up and throw haymakers. *Okay, I can do that too*, I thought. *Fuck it. Let's play Rock 'Em Sock 'Em Robots.* I started letting my fists fly from my left and right, then, *BLAP!* I threw a left hand that started in Japan and worked its way to Vegas, which put Wanderlei on his ass, out cold. I followed up with a right-hand square to his face that bounced his head off the canvas like a basketball, and the ref was finally able to stop the fight, which officially ended Wanderlei's middleweight reign. I yelled out, "Fuck yeah," as confetti rained down.

I became the first double-weight champion in MMA history, but at the time, I didn't know how big of a feat that was. On top of that, Wanderlei had to give me his middleweight belt. Pride, unlike the UFC, wasn't making a new belt each time there was a title fight, so, to this day, I have that belt on my wall, right next to my welterweight brass.

People today are shocked to find out that it was me, not Conor McGregor, who was the first "champ champ" or "double champ" in a major mixed martial arts promotion. My buddy Randy had won belts in different weight classes in the UFC, but never at the same time. It wasn't until Conor went to the UFC and won the featherweight and lightweight titles simultaneously that I realized what I had done was nearly impossible to do. The difference is, I was never vocal about what I did. I didn't need to pat myself on the back. Maybe I should've, but that wasn't my style. There were some guys in the UFC that had tried to do it before but had fallen short. So when Conor was able to achieve double-champ status in 2016, I thought it was a cool thing. Difference was, Conor tooted his own horn. He's his biggest fan.

It was good he brought more attention to the sport and the whole double-champ thing, but *I* was the one to do it first. Had I beaten Big Nog, I would've been a triple champ, the first and only "champ champ champ." I personally don't think a three-weight division champ will ever be done. Boxers are able to win belts in different weight classes frequently, but there's so many damn belts and weight classes for boxers to achieve those goals. It irked me a bit to know that if I had beaten Big Nog, I would have been the only fighter to hold three belts at once. It wasn't meant to be, but I was still glad to be a part of MMA world champion history.

★★★
11

PRIDEFUL DOWNFALL | UFC PART DEUX

"Breaking News. UFC to buy Pride Fighting Championships."
In March 2007, I was at the gym training when I saw this
headline pop up on my phone. I didn't know if it was a joke or if
there was merit to the headline. As soon as I got home, I hopped on
the internet to see what the fuck this was all about.

It was true; Pride was selling their promotion and entire library
of fights to the UFC. I had no idea this was coming. I had just made
my biggest purse to date, $300,000 for my win over Wanderlei,
and was waiting for a call from Pride with a new fight offer. It
never came.

———————————

I had first met Frank Fertitta, Lorenzo Fertitta, and Dana White
in April 2001. The only thing I knew was that the Fertittas were
casino owners and Dana was a boxing aerobics instructor who
used to manage Chuck Liddell and Tito Ortiz. In January 2001,
their company, Zuffa, had bought the UFC from SEG for $2 mil-
lion. That may seem like a lot of money to some people, but the
Fertittas and Dana knew the sport was dying in America.

Mixed martial arts was struggling to get off the ground because
of all the legislation against the sport and the athletic commissions
not sanctioning fights nationwide. At times, fights were put on

at Indian reservations to get around this. There were only a few places the UFC could take fight cards at the time, and slowly, cable distributors started to shy away from showing their PPVs. It was so bad, none of the major news outlets would cover it. It was only a matter of time before the UFC would have to fold.

The first time I met the three of them was before I cornered Randy for his fight at UFC 31. They had had their first card as the Zuffa brand a few months before at Donald Trump's Taj Mahal in Atlantic City in February 2001; it was one of the few venues that welcomed MMA fights. Trump was also one of the few major supporters of mixed martial arts in the pioneer days and has always supported the right for fighters to be able to make a living in the cage or ring. This was an unpopular opinion then, but Trump didn't care. He advocated for mixed martial arts to be accepted by the mainstream powers that be.

Lorenzo and Frank were nice and professional. Dana was the same, but more importantly, I could tell these guys wanted the sport to take off. At the core, they were still businessmen, but there was a genuineness to them. They had a vision for the sport after seeing a gap in the combat-sports market.

I was halfway into my first Pride contract when Dana and the Fertittas expressed interest in signing me, but when I told them my fight purses, they got quiet. They weren't paying most fighters close to what I was making, and they would end those talks by saying, "Just let us know when your contract is over," but there were no other discussions at that time.

Over the years, many people have asked me about my relationship with Dana. It wasn't overly complicated. Initially, he wasn't my boss, so I would joke around with him when I saw him, tease him that his hair was thinning out or about his weight. It was all in good fun, and he laughed the jokes off and kept things professional.

In September 2002, they held UFC 39, and during fight week they went out of their way to be hospitable and put me up in my own room at the Mohegan Sun in Connecticut. I was in town helping Randy, who was once again fighting for the heavyweight belt. I had lunch with Lorenzo and Dana that fight week, and they mentioned that it would be great if I fought for UFC again, but they never made me an offer. Every time numbers came up, and I told them what I was making (by my fourth Pride fight I was over $100,000), they never followed up. I understood it was just business. They were trying to keep the UFC afloat, and my salary was out of the ballpark for them. On the one hand, you had the Fertittas and Dana shelling out cash to make sure the thing didn't fold, while in Japan, MMA was flourishing. It was a tale of two cites.

The end of that fight week didn't go so well for us. Randy lost and got his orbital bone broken. He had to have surgery right away where they put a mesh covering over the fracture so the muscle wouldn't get caught when he moved it.

A couple years after the Zuffa buy, I could see they had done a great job in achieving acceptance of the sport in the States. Then, Dana came up to me at a UFC event and was excited as fuck when we started chatting. I was still doing well in Pride, on one of my four-fight win streaks, so we were just shooting the shit.

"Dan, I think this is going to pretty big for the sport," Dana said. "It's definitely going to get us more attention at minimum. There's this new network that's willing to take a chance on us and broadcast us on fuckin' cable!"

Dana told me that Spike TV was looking for new content. The UFC had come up with a concept show where two UFC stars coach two teams of fighters. The fighters must live in one house for the duration of the show and fight in a tournament to earn a contract. And for the grand finale, the two coaches would fight each other on a PPV card or major event.

I thought Dana's idea was badass and hoped it would blow mixed martial arts up even more in the United States. I was fighting at the peak of Pride, but I thought competition was good. At the end of the day, UFC growing could only help fighters. More fans meant more advertisers and more money.

When the show came out in 2005, they called it *The Ultimate Fighter* (*TUF*). The first season had Randy and Chuck coaching opposite each other, which culminated in a rematch at UFC 52. The show did great. *TUF* put up huge viewership numbers that were beyond what the brass projected.

Diego Sanchez beat Kenny Florian in a middleweight matchup, and then there was the epic slugfest between Forrest Griffin and Stephan Bonnar, which made the world take notice of the UFC brand. After that, I saw the UFC start to gain popularity quickly, with people in Japan and the rest of the world being able to see clips on the internet.

Before the UFC was able to get *TUF* on television, there weren't many people internationally who could see UFC fights. Pride was the promotion that was accessible for people to watch overseas, which was one of the main reasons why Pride was much more popular at the time. *TUF* was the catalyst for helping start the UFC's international brand recognition.

Dana had told me they were losing a lot of money before the Spike deal and were close to calling it quits. The Ferttitas couldn't keep funneling money into the brand if it wasn't going to flip and make a profit. I don't know how close to being done they were, or how long they could've sustained if they didn't get *TUF* on Spike, but I was glad it started to propel them.

RIIIIING—
"Hey, Randy."

"I heard the news," Randy said. "No more Pride?"

"I don't know. That's the way it looks."

I was still reeling in shock from the announcement, but I did know Pride was having some difficulty. And it had *nothing* to do with their fights. There were rumors that Pride had some alleged mafia ties, and the accusations were coming in from multiple fronts. The media was starting to allege this, and another one of Pride's rivals, K-1, was involved in a smear campaign against Pride as well. Some sponsors dropped out, but Pride kept putting on shows, so I thought nothing of it.

Did the mafia allegations have any merit? I don't know. I'm sure all of the promotions out there were connected to the mafia in some way, but I never saw it in Pride. I would see the mafia figures show up in smaller promotions when I was coaching other fighters, but there was none of this with Pride. But when Fuji TV canceled their Pride contract in June 2006, I knew it wasn't a good thing. I fought twice after that, so figured it was business as usual.

In hindsight, business was unstable, it was just none of the fighters knew. It became apparent because there was only one more Pride event after my knockout in Pride 33 over Wanderlei, and the rest was history when UFC bought Pride and their whole library for around $70 million. Talk about a quick turnaround. The UFC went from almost going under two years before to buying their biggest rival. Now that's a master comeback.

When the UFC contacted me about my deal, they initially thought they owned my Pride contract, but that wasn't the case. Once again, California law said it wasn't valid for them to own my contract, which gave me the freedom to negotiate a new deal. I was one of Pride's superstars and had two championship belts in hand.

UFC gave me a new contract and bumped up my pay, which included possibilities of bonuses and pay-per-view (PPV) bonuses for certain fights or if I became champ. Usually, the UFC contracts are performance-based. Most fighters get 50 percent of their money to show up and 50 percent to win. My deal was around 80 percent to show and 20 percent to win, with my final pay for each fight being greater than my Pride deal. It can be confusing as fuck, but my basic math could tell if a number was bigger or smaller than the other.

———————

I signed my deal in Summer 2007 and was officially back in the UFC. It had been just over nine years since I had won the UFC Middleweight Tournament, and this time, I was set to fight Rampage Jackson for the UFC Light Heavyweight Championship. Rampage had spent five years in Pride then one fight in the World Fighting Alliance before the UFC purchased Pride and Rampage joined their ranks. I had known him by his first name, Quinton, for the most part because of our Pride days, and we had trained together a few years before. I would go to Tiki Ghosn's gym to train with Quinton, Tito Ortiz, and other guys in Huntington Beach, California, when I lived there. I grappled and sparred with Quinton, er, Rampage, and thought he was a good dude. He had a sense of humor, and we had a mutual respect for each other. In fact, a year and a half before we were supposed to fight, we were on the hit show *King of Queens* together.

———————

RIIIIIING!

"Dan, what's your schedule like next month?"

It was Ryan Parsons, one of my cornermen who I had known since my ASU days. He had walked on to the wrestling team, and we were roommates for a bit in Huntington Beach. Ryan had become a chiropractor, nutritionist, and trainer. Had I gone to chiropractor school, I would have enrolled with him.

"I don't know. Why, what's up?" I said.

"They want to bring you and some of the guys on the show," Ryan said.

"Who?"

"Kevin. *King of Queens*. They wrote a bit in one of their episodes."

Ryan had told me he was introduced to Kevin James (I think Bas Rutten did the introduction), the star of *King of Queens*. Ryan had worked with him a little bit, and he told me Kevin was a huge MMA fan. I knew Kevin was familiar with the sport, I had met him a few times before with his whole writing crew, and they seemed to be cool people. But I didn't think they loved mixed martial arts to the point of using real fighters on a hit network show. I was honored to be one of the guys they wanted. Randy, Rampage, and Frank Trigg were the other three, so I said yes.

I had a blast on set, and it was an unforgettable experience. Kevin's character was looking to fight a couple of rival guys when he had a flashback. It was me, Randy, Frank, and Rampage looking at him and his crew, mean-mugging them. Kevin threw a right hook and hit me in the face, then I smiled and took out my flipper teeth. I grabbed him, kneed him a couple times, then threw him on the ground. You'll only see me throw him once, but I had to do that shit like ten to fifteen times, and Kevin wasn't the lightest guy.

What I respected about Kevin was he didn't have a stand-in or stunt guy switch places with him during the throws. Every stunt was done by him. Hell, if Kevin wasn't a movie star, he probably could've fought in MMA like he did in his role for the film *Here Comes the Boom*.

The UFC had brought me to Vegas to watch Rampage fight Chuck in May, just three months after my knockout of Wanderlei, and their plan was for me to fight the winner. I didn't care who I fought; I knew both of them. I had trained and partied with Chuck a couple times and spent a little more time with Rampage. And Rampage did his part—he went out there and knocked Chuck out, which I think was the beginning of Chuck's chin going downhill.

Following the knockout, the UFC officials brought me in the cage with both of my Pride belts in hand and had Joe Rogan interview me and Rampage. Rampage was joking and trying to get me to take my flipper out, but I was just excited to get ready for our fight, which I thought was a win for the fans. It would be a match between the UFC and Pride champions in the light heavyweight division. We would be fighting in the brand-new O2 Arena in London, England. I knew the British were big into MMA, and seventeen thousand passionate fans showed up at UFC 75.

Rampage was one of the guys who would try and get inside his opponents' heads, but since we knew each other, there were no pre-fight antics from him. That shit didn't work with me anyways, but there was also a high level of respect that we had for each other's fighting abilities. Because he respected my skills, I was certain that I would be getting the best Quinton "Rampage" Jackson that anyone had ever seen in the cage. And I was 100 percent right; that's exactly what I got. He came into the fight in peak condition mentally, physically, and probably spiritually too. I had seen him go into other dangerous fights not as focused and a little heavy, out of shape. But not for this one, and I wouldn't want anyone but at their best. He knew all eyes would be on us, and we would be in for a dogfight.

The fight was much closer than how the judges scored it, and I thought I had done enough to win the fight. If it was Pride rules, the judges there scored fights based upon the totality of the fight and not round by round. A fighter couldn't win on just points if he was almost finished in the fight with no offensive recourse. There's zero doubt that my hand would've been raised in Pride, but it wasn't; the judges gave him the win. I was disappointed, but I learned some valuable lessons that night.

I didn't know how big of a change fighting in a cage was going to be. It wasn't difficult going from the cage to the ring, but the other way around fucked with me a little bit. I had Quinton in some fucked-up positions, which would've been devastating for him if we were in Pride. One was a crucifix, which is a position where both of your opponent's arms are completely trapped and that fighter is basically screwed. The lack of training in a cage made me forget that since we were near the cage fence, he could use his feet on the cage to help him get up and out of the situation. If that had been in Pride, I would've been raining punches on him. Hindsight is 20/20, but if I had remembered he could do that then it would've been fairly easy to scoot him away from it. It had been almost a decade since I had fought in a cage, and I had been an infant at MMA then. And, without a cage, there were some positions I couldn't train in.

The other difference were the rounds. I was used to the first round being ten minutes, not five, and a lot can happen without a one-minute break. Some fighters aren't able to sustain as well in Pride's longer rounds, but my conditioning had adapted to it. Those long rounds are what separated the men from the boys. Rampage was smart and had learned from his previous losses. He had been knocked out by Wanderlei twice and Shogun once in a span of six fights in Pride, so I think he understood how to utilize the Octagon by not getting cornered and forced into a firefight. The square formation of the ring forced fighters to engage or be trapped in a corner. The cage allows fighters to keep circling around the Octagon.

The ring is more fan friendly. They're able to see the action easier, whereas the cage is much harder viewing because of the fencing. Also, during the fight, I tripped a couple of times on the bottom outskirts of the cage, which the ring didn't have, when Rampage was throwing a punch. That shit didn't look too good because judges might have seen my knockdown as a result of the punch, which wasn't the case.

There is no doubt that fighting in a ring is overall more difficult, because you need to be technically sound and ready to engage. A cage is fine, it just gives fighters with less skill the ability to run away from action. I'm not taking anything away from Quinton, but if we had fought with Pride rules in the cage, it would've been scored differently.

It always sucked to lose, but after the fight, I figured I would stay at 205 pounds. I knew 185 pounds was the more natural weight class for me, but I thought I could beat anyone at light heavyweight. I wanted a rematch with Rampage for the belt since the fight was close, but Dana announced at the end of 2007 that he would be fighting Forrest Griffin after they coached *TUF* 7. Their fight wouldn't happen until July 2008, so when the New Year came around, I was trying to weigh my options, and then I got the call from my manager, Jordan Feagan.

"Hello?"

"Hey, they want you to fight in March, Dan."

"Who?"

"Anderson. At one eighty-five for the title."

Anderson "The Spider" Silva was another Pride veteran who had strung together six straight wins. Take out the DQ he had for an illegal kick, and he would've had nine wins in a row.

"Okay, I'll do it."

I knew Anderson was going to be tough, but I also knew I was going to have to cut weight for this fight. When I fought at 205, I'd usually weigh in around 200 pounds, but it had been about two years since I cut down to 185. I was getting older as well. I was less than six months from my thirty-seventh birthday, so I knew cutting weight wasn't going to be as easy.

I ended up not having the best weight cut for the fight. I had to tip the scales at an even 185 pounds. If it were a non-title fight, I could've come in a pound over, but sometimes that last pound can be the hardest. On top of that, when you're cutting weight, and there's not much fat to come off, you're basically just sucking all the water out of your body. The body starts to dehydrate, which isn't good for getting punched in the head.

My fight with Anderson was slated for UFC 82 on March 1, 2008. We had two previous opponents in common. Fans and experts are constantly trying to do MMA Math and predict fights based on past opponents, but it doesn't always pan out.

We had both defeated Carlos Newton but had had much different outcomes against Ryo Chonan. I had obliterated him in less than thirty seconds, and Anderson was taken out by him. Ryo used a sparsely used submission, a flying scissor heel hook, on Anderson and forced him to tap. I knew our fight wasn't going to end that way. I wasn't going to do any flying ninja shit and doubted Anderson would try the same.

"Fight!"

The ref beckoned us to battle, and I tried to touch gloves with him, but Anderson didn't want to touch. *Okay, whatever.* I wasn't pissed off about it, maybe I should've been, but those first couple minutes we were cautious. Both of us were trying to figure out the other's timing, until we eventually exchanged some punches and kicks.

For some reason, I felt flat during my pre-fight warmups. I got rid of negative thoughts that crept into my head, and I felt okay at the start of the fight. In the first round, I was able to take him down and get some ground-and-pound punches, but I wasn't close to finishing him. In the second round, I had a body lock but didn't attempt to take him down as my arms felt fatigued. Anderson also made some minor adjustments and was pretty slick on his feet. It was hard for me to time him, and oddly enough I wasn't adjusting to his movements.

I wasn't sure if it was due to the weight cut, but I didn't have the laser vision, the Spidey sense I usually had, and got caught with a big kick from Anderson. He threw some punches that didn't do much, but as soon as I fully recovered, *boom!* I got knocked to the ground silly. Again I tried to recover and grabbed his wrist to avoid strikes before standing up. I had my bearings about me, but I lost control of his wrist, and he caught me with a good shot. Anderson then took my back and threw some punches and elbows to my head until he was able to flatten me out, and he sunk in a rear naked choke with eight seconds left in the second round.

We got Fight of the Night honors and bonus money for the match, but I was pissed at myself for not feeling 100 percent. I wanted to get another crack at him while I was at my best. Once again, I had dropped two fights in a row. That shit sucked, but the greater hurt was in the ways I had lost.

I knew how long it had taken to get a rematch with Wanderlei, but I was never able to avenge the Rampage and Anderson losses. I was surprised when news broke in 2015 that Anderson had gotten popped for two anabolic steroids, Drostanolone and Androstane. He had tested positive before and after the fight and was suspended, then he got busted in 2018 by USADA for taking a supplement with other banned substances. I doubt he fought me clean.

I wasn't mad, because how could I be? Most fighters were using that shit in Pride and probably the UFC before the more stringent testing came along. Did my opponents being on steroids help give them an edge? I don't fuckin' know. Maybe.

Anderson wasn't the first guy I fought in my career to do 'roids. Vitor was the only one who I fought and who got busted afterwards. I had no control over what other people did or didn't do. I try not to think about it too much, but it has to put a question mark on their entire careers.

But other sports have the same fuckin' problem. Our sport was different, though, where you don't *play* fighting. If the testing of today was around when I started, some of those fighters would not have the same legacy today. I'm not making excuses for my losses or even fighting on an unfair playing field because I'd still fight anyone or anybody, even if I knew they were juicing. No questions asked. Ring or cage, I would've gotten in there and put my life on the line because I believed in myself, my skills, and my ability to beat their asses, regardless of what they were sticking in them.

☆☆☆
12

BEATING ANOTHER UFC CHAMP |
GOOD NIGHT, MICHAEL BISPING!

Everybody loves a good fight. Just go to YouTube and read the comments on some random street fights. People turn into Joe Rogan and give their non-expert opinion like, "Those guys suck, they're both losers," or, "I would beat both their asses." There's a ton of internet trolls. I'm slow to criticize anybody, because I know what it takes to get thrown in a ring or locked in a cage. I just wanted to fight in the best promotions against the greatest fighters on the planet.

After my second fight back in the UFC, I knew both promotions put on great fights, but Pride put on these fantastic, elaborate shows. *Boom, boom,* fireworks would explode in calculated pyrotechnic shows that captivated the crowd. Smoke plumes floated like mist in all the right directions. Choreographed ceremonies on elaborate set designs took the audience back to the samurai days. And those sets changed for each event. A Pride fight card wasn't merely a show, it was an experience. Shit, the money they put into those productions was worth the price of admission alone.

In professional sports, you're only as good as your last win. It's cliché to say, but there's a shitload of truth in this, especially in fighting.

Everybody loves a winner. But a loser? In boxing, you better not lose. Unless you're Muhammad Ali or Mike Tyson, fans and media look at a loss the same way people look at a plague. They don't want anything to do with it. It's fuckin' stupid to think a fighter's legacy or greatness is based purely upon wins and losses. Mixed martial arts isn't quite the same, but it can be. Fans only remember if you're the champ. Being a fun, exciting fighter will only take you so far in MMA, because at some point, you better fuckin' win, especially in America. So when I lost two straight fights after returning to the UFC, it sucked balls, but what could I do? I just needed a win. But I wasn't in the driver's seat, the UFC was.

When I got a call from my manager a couple months after the Anderson fight to say they wanted me to fight at UFC 88 in September, I knew it wouldn't be for a title, but I figured it would at least be against some household name, maybe former UFC Middleweight Champ Rich Franklin, or Chuck Liddell. That would sell some PPVs.

"Who do they want me to fight?" I asked.

He paused, so I knew both of my guesses were wrong. "I've never heard of him. You probably haven't either." He had said enough.

I knew from his tone I wasn't going to be the main event or get a percentage of PPV buys. Still, I needed a win. "Okay, that's fine with me."

If it was up to me, I would never fight a no-name. What good does that do me? Losing back-to-back fights in mixed martial arts doesn't look good. Fighting is not like the NFL. The Dallas Cowboys can lose eight games in a season and still win the Super Bowl. In mixed martial arts, losing too many fights in a short time span will probably cost you your job. I had to work my way back up having not won a fight in a year and a half. If I lost three straight, I couldn't use the cage as an excuse anymore. Not that I did. I just tried to stay positive. I thought, *I can't lose this.*

Rousimar Palhares, another Brazilian BJJ black belt, wound up being the guy they put in front of me in Atlanta during Labor Day weekend. I Googled Rousimar to see who he was and what type of fighter I'd be facing. Before going to war, you're doing yourself a disservice if you don't research your enemy. What are their strengths? Weaknesses? Rousimar was a submission specialist and had a pretty impressive record with some nasty leg submissions. I saw some fights when he had a submission locked on his opponent. The guy would tap, and this motherfucker would hold his death grip a little longer and try to tear ligaments or break a leg, even after the ref jumped in to stop the fight. I wasn't too worried about his submissions. I just needed to be mindful of them. For that whole training camp, I worked on nothing but leg locks.

The fight played out the same way I had envisioned it. I dropped him with some hard punches, but I didn't want to be reckless and jump on him. That's what he wanted, and his ass tried to stay on the ground and goad me into a grappling match. I was like, *Fuck that*. I wasn't going to be stupid and engage him where he was at his best. I made the ref stand him up so I could knock his ass back down again. The fight continued that way for three rounds. He would shoot in for a takedown and try to grab one of my legs. A couple of times he succeeded and had two or three good submission attempts, but I was able to defend well and get back to my feet. It wasn't the most exciting fight I've had, but if we had stayed on our feet, I would've knocked him the fuck out. I was just glad to get the *W* and put my losses behind me.

Rousimar went on to infamy. After our match, he became a dirtier fighter and held on to submissions even longer than before. I lost all respect for him. He was another fighter who tried to feed his inflated ego. I probably should've tried harder to separate his head from his consciousness. I wasn't surprised when the UFC permanently kicked him out in 2013 for his disgusting tactics. The year before, he was suspended for elevated testosterone levels. I have to say the fucker looked like he was on a healthy dose of steroids when I fought him.

The fight game is a lot like gambling. There's an unpredictable nature to it. One moment you're down, the next you're a winner in everyone's eyes again. You might get a call for a fight right away, or the phone could go silent. It's like Russian roulette, and I wasn't getting younger. At thirty-eight years old, an age most fighters are considered over the hill, I still wanted to be world champion again. I felt like I had a ton of fight in me still.

Shortly after my win over Rousimar, in late 2008, I saw my new Android phone light up. It was Dana. I said, "What's up," expecting him to offer me a name or two for my next fight. That wasn't the first thing on his mind.

"Hey, how do you feel about coaching *TUF*?"

That was weird. I didn't expect him to ask me that, but it seemed okay to me. "Fine. I'd like it," I said.

I could tell Dana was pleased. "Great. We want you to fight Rich in January, and the winner will coach opposite Bisping. We're going to do *TUF* a little different this season. Instead of picking teams, it's going to be Team USA versus Team UK. We really want to tap into the European market and think this will do some numbers."

I had heard other fighters grumble about coaching on *TUF*, while others have just flat out said no. Maybe it was the money. At the time, the UFC was paying head coaches $600 a week, less for assistants. The pay didn't bother me. I thought it would be fun to coach on the show because it pushed the notoriety of the fighters to a bigger market on television. It was free advertising for me. I had had enough contracts to know that wider recognition led to greater pay. It's the fans that pay for the tickets to the venue, order the PPVs, and buy merchandise. So why not? Besides, I loved to coach. I didn't mind helping someone figure out a way to beat someone else's ass.

The UFC flew me and Rich out to Dublin, Ireland, a day earlier, and the following day we flew on Zuffa's private jet to England to watch the Team UK tryouts. UFC middleweight contender Michael "The Count" Bisping was there to see the fighters he would be coaching, while Rich and I were there to scope out our potential competition. After the tryouts, we headed back to Dublin. When I got there, it felt like Antarctica. It was *cold* as fuck. Even the gym I trained at during fight week was freezing. Usually, I would train barefoot, but the mats felt like I was walking on a frozen pond, so I went to the mall and bought the warmest socks Dublin offered to train in.

It was the first (and last) time I fought in Dublin, and what I loved is how energetic the Irish fans were. They had some really passionate MMA fans. And the crowd was shockingly loud. There were only about ten thousand people in attendance, but it sounded like a hundred thousand fans cheering me and Rich on like we were in medieval times. Rich had become UFC champ after Murilo Bustamante vacated the belt to join Pride. I didn't know Rich personally, but he was respectful and seemed like a nice guy. I had seen some of his previous fights and didn't think he was that dangerous for my style.

All the niceness got thrown out the door when I made my walk out to the cage. I was like Mel Gibson in *Braveheart* when I heard the Irish fans screaming. All that was missing was a horse and spear. I had my sword, though; it was the power in my hands. I knew Rich's sword wasn't heavier than mine, and I was ready for our duel.

I was right. In the fight, there were a few times where I unloaded my right hand and hurt him pretty good, but Rich was a tough dude, and he was able to weather the storm. He even caught me with a few good knees, but I was never hurt, and I won by split decision.

After the fight, the media asked me about the judge who thought Rich won 30–27. I didn't know what the fuck he was thinking. I was just glad it hadn't affected the outcome. With MMA judges, you never know. You don't know what they're thinking, how they are scoring the fight, or who they have up on the cards. There's no transparency until the scorecards are read, and worse, there's no explanation if the judges fuck up a decision.

It would be beneficial to fighters, their corners, and fans if there was live scoring, meaning their scores were released after every round. It might also help if there were more real, veteran fighters who were retired that judged the fights. That would lead to less fighters getting screwed out of winning, which can be devastating both mentally and financially. A fucked-up loss can set you back a couple years from a title shot. Even worse, a fighter may never get a championship bout due to injuries, bad matchups, contract disputes, or age.

When I got back to California, I stayed there for a couple days, then headed straight to Vegas to film *TUF*. It was a little weird that I knew who my opponent was so far in advance, but my approach to the fight was the same—find out what Bisping was all about. From what I had seen of him, he acted like a fuckin' prick.

At UFC 75, he was fighting in the co-main event against Matt Hamill. While I was warming up for my fight against Rampage, I watched their fight from the locker room. Bisping had been taken down throughout the fight, with Matt able to ground and pound him. The only problem was the fight took place in London, and the judges gifted the win to the Englishman, Bisping, by split decision. At the post-fight conference, a British reporter asked Bisping if he agreed with the decision. Instead of answering the question he said, "Fuck you, let's go to the parking lot. I'll beat your fuckin' ass!" I was shocked by how he represented the sport then. Another reporter tried to ask him the same thing in a different manner but got a similar response. I thought Bisping was an asshole at best, and at worst, a fuckin' douchebag. I did respect him for being who he was on and off the camera. He *is* that guy. There's a ton of fakes and phonies who have a persona on camera then act completely different when the cameras aren't rolling. Bisping didn't change. He was a douche regardless.

When Dana introduced me to Team USA, it was a badass moment. I was proud to coach the Americans against another country, but I appreciated, too, what he said. "This is Team USA versus Team UK. And obviously your coach this season is going to be Dan Henderson, one of the greatest fighters ever in mixed martial arts history. And he's one of the toughest motherfuckers I've ever met in my life."

That season there were two weight divisions, lightweight and welterweight. There were two fights each week, and it was filmed over a six-week period. The *TUF* format is genius. All the fighters had to stay under one roof, and besides training, they weren't able to leave the house or communicate with the outside world. The two winners get a UFC contract. Sounds easy? You had to win four straight fights rooming with a bunch of strangers. Plenty of people lose their shit on the show.

Bisping tried to get under my skin while filming. It didn't work; I was my usual self. Like Teddy Roosevelt: "Speak softly and carry a big stick." I'm the same laid-back person whether someone gets in my face or not. Bisping still tried. In one instance, my guys wanted to switch practices from mornings to afternoons, which production allowed midway through filming. I let Bisping know our decision after practice, "Hey, my guys want to switch up, so next week we'll take afternoons." Instead of saying, "Okay," he made a huge ordeal over it. I heard he had been partying late, so his bitch ass didn't want to switch to mornings. He said, "Whoever wins the next fight, that determines if we switch or not." I told him no, but then he said, "Oh, are you scared? You don't have faith your fighter can beat mine?"

None of those tactics worked with me. I was out late partying too, but could still handle my shit, so his shenanigans just made him look worse. Not only that, but he missed one or two fights because he was sleeping in after a long night out. That showed a complete lack of respect for his fighters. I was disappointed that one of my guys didn't win the show, but I was there for them every step of the way. And when Dana did the coaches' challenge, which was tennis that season, I made sure to beat Bisping's ass. I had never played tennis, and absolutely sucked at it, but I wanted to win some money for the Team USA guys and shut Bisping up. After I won 6–2, Bisping said, "Wait until we get in the cage, Dan."

I just smiled and said, "I can't wait." I think he thought the shit talking was going to give him an edge. Maybe he was simply trying to hype himself up. He acted like a child, so I didn't pay him much attention. Bisping's words weren't going to change the way I planned on fighting him. He should've been wary of what he couldn't see. My mental toughness.

After we wrapped filming, Dana took both teams out to a fancy restaurant, then a club with bottle service. He even gave out some casino chips to take care of the guys. My relationship with Dana had changed over the years, but it was still okay. I told him I was in the market for a new car, and he had a Range Rover I was thinking about purchasing. "How do you like the car?" I asked when we were filming. He tossed me the keys to his car and said, "Try it out for yourself. Keep it for a few days." After I drove it around, he asked me what I thought. I liked it and told him I would probably buy one for myself. I didn't have to. At the end of the season, he bought me and Bisping brand-new Range Rovers.

My fight with Bisping was the final fight on that contract and was set to be the co-main event at UFC 100. The main event was Georges St-Pierre defending his UFC Welterweight Championship belt against Thiago Alves. Or so I thought. It didn't happen that way. My fight got bumped to third on the main card, and the UFC booked the heavyweights to take center stage.

WWE superstar Brock Lesnar had crossed over into real fighting and had beaten Randy the year before to win the UFC Heavyweight Championship. I thought he had the potential to eventually become a UFC star, but I thought it was fucked up that someone with a 2–1 record was able to get a title shot that quickly. Why was he deserving to skip the line of fighters who had been waiting? It wasn't personal, Brock was dedicated to mixed martial arts; one of his MMA coaches was Marty Morgan, the same guy I beat in overtime at the 1996 Olympic Trials. But now I got bumped down so he could face former UFC Heavyweight Champion Frank Mir.

The two were supposed to fight at UFC 98, but Frank had gotten hurt and the UFC re-booked it. Under normal circumstances, I would have been fine fighting third, but my contract only gave me a part of the PPV money if I was the main or co-main event.

The UFC did a great job marketing and promoting their one hundredth PPV event. Fight week was filled with media who were intrigued about my matchup with loudmouth Bisping. All twelve episodes of *TUF* had been broadcast, which brought in more viewers and a bigger fanbase. The media and fans wanted to know if I could shut the young bull Bisping up, whose stock was on the rise with this 17–1 record. Then there was GSP, one of the all-time greats, who was not just a fan favorite, but a good dude overall. And Brock was the icing on the cake. He brought over an enormous following from WWE by staying in his wrestling character. Brock put on the persona of an angry, untamed animal that couldn't be beaten or fucked with. It worked for his brand.

After all the media and hoopla, my ass still had to go out there and fight. On July 11, 2009, I felt confident as I walked into the cage. I had a ton of time to prepare for Bisping. My mind had downloaded all the information I needed to fight him. I knew that anything could happen. He could get lucky and land a wild punch. But my childhood lessons taught me if you respect your opponent and their skills, there's less chance of you overlooking shit. Bisping had over a dozen knockouts, but most of them were from an accumulation of punches. He didn't have a metal fist like me but was still a skilled fighter. It was his cardio that helped him outlast his opponents. He would keep the same pace in fights and tire them out right before finishing them. Unfortunately for him, his style was good for me.

Blam, blam! I hit Bisping with some awesome shots in the first round, and after he felt my power, he shot for a takedown from a mile away. When the horn sounded the end of the round, I smiled thinking, *This motherfucker is trying to wrestle me?* In the second round, I just stalked him. I didn't think he could hurt me. Bisping hit me with some punches, but after I felt his power, my respect for his striking went down. I continued forward and *whew!* I just missed rearranging his face with my right hand. Seconds later, he made the fatal mistake of moving to his left, and right into maybe the cleanest, hardest overhand right in MMA history. *Baaaaam!* I threw an inside leg kick then ducked my head down, and I connected with every ounce of power I had onto the left side of Bisping's jaw. *Boop!* His mouthpiece went flying into the stands, and he was out dreaming in la-la land before his head hit the canvas. I wanted to finish the job, so before referee Mario Yamasaki stopped the fight, I was already in the air with another follow-up punch, and I landed another right hand to his face to make sure he didn't wake up prematurely. The roar from the crowd was deafening. I was the Gladiator once again. Maximus Meridius had conquered Commodus.

To this day, the UFC has put my finish of Bisping as one of the "greatest knockouts of all time," and I still get asked about the follow-up punch. "Dan, was that follow-up punch necessary? Don't you think it was excessive?" I said the same thing then that I say now. "No way." I tell everyone to look at my previous knockouts. I kept going until the ref stopped the fight. Bisping wasn't the first. There just happened to be a lot more eyes on that event. It wasn't even personal. The media took some of my words out of context in my post-fight interview with Joe Rogan. "Maybe that'll shut him up, but I don't think it will." But my intent wasn't to permanently incapacitate him, just temporarily. And it worked. After the fight, Bisping didn't know what the fuck had happened. Some of our mutual friends told me he thought we were still filming *TUF*. He didn't remember the fight or knockout. I'm glad he was able to get up and walk out on his own accord, but there is no love in war.

I'll never forget that event for many reasons, and I celebrated with my whole crew in Vegas for the next couple of days and nights. Ironically, when I headed back to California in my brand-new Range Rover, it took a shitter on the side of the freeway and broke down. I was like, *What the fuck?!* I tweeted a photo of the Range on a tow truck bed on a brand-new social media platform called Twitter. (Little did I know that Twitter would sell over a decade later for $44 billion! I was in the wrong business.)

Every time I'm in a new city, at least one person will approach me and say, "Thank you for knocking out Bisping." I don't tell them I didn't do it for them specifically. I just smile and shake their hand. I would've knocked him out even if he was a nice guy. Hell, if Big Bird signed a contract to try and beat my ass, then I'd have to put down one big bird.

13

PAY ME, DANA | WORLD CHAMP AGAIN

One of the things my dad indirectly taught me and my brother was to stand up for ourselves. He didn't mean for us to be rude or throw shit in other people's faces, but not stand back, even when it comes to my thoughts. If I feel slighted or any bit of miscommunication, I might not say them publicly, but I will talk to you man to man. And I won't forget our conversation either. I have the memory of an elephant.

I gave Dana a call a few weeks before my fight with Bisping to see if I would still get a share of PPV buys since I was originally promoted as the co-main event, which meant additional money if the card did well. "Dana, I know what my contract says, but you guys have been promoting this thing like I'm one of the main attractions."

Dana didn't budge. "Your contract states you only get pay-per-view revenue on main and co-main. I don't know what to tell you."

Who made those rules? "Why can't you do two co-main fights? I don't get it. My face is plastered on all the UFC 100 marketing posters and shit."

"Nope, sorry, Dan, you won't get a piece of this one."

That was it. I wasn't going to argue with him, but I thought after the fight, Dana might do the right thing and give me a bonus. I knew he had given out locker room bonuses in the past, especially if a show did well, and UFC 100 did huge numbers with 1.6 million PPV buys. I did get $100,000 for Knockout of the Night, but that was for the outcome, not my services. All in I got paid a few hundred thousand for the fight. If the UFC had paid me for PPV buys, it would have been for more than $3.5 million. The event was a smashing success and still one of the top grossing PPVs in history. If Dana had been cool after the fight and said, "You know what, we probably should've kicked you down something since you were supposed to get PPV, but I'm going to give you a little bonus anyways," I would've been happy with that. But he didn't, and that affected how I went into negotiating my next contract.

After my fight with Bisping, Rich Franklin was supposed to fight someone in Dallas two months later, but something happened and the UFC called me to do a new deal. It had only been a couple weeks after UFC 100, so I told them I didn't want to fight him since I had just beaten him, but if the price was right, I would do it.

The UFC announced the fight with Rich before we had even agreed to a deal, a tactic they will do to try and force the hand of a fighter, but I wanted to be paid what I thought I was worth. Initially, they agreed to the money I asked for but not sponsorships and other things that accumulated to my all-in asking price. They countered with another offer, and we were close to a deal, but they wouldn't agree to all the nuances.

The UFC needed time to promote a fight with Rich, so Dana put on his business hat and told the media the fight with Rich and I was canceled because fans didn't want it. That was complete bullshit. I went back to the UFC and asked them to pay me what would be equivalent to $800,000 per fight with bonuses and PPV money. It wouldn't be guaranteed, I would need to win and perform well to be paid this. They said no and countered with about half. I thanked them and told them I thought my value was more, so I reached out to a newer promotion, Strikeforce. I spoke to their CEO, Scott Coker, and found that they were easier to deal with.

"Do you really want to fight for us, or are you trying to inflate your asking price from the UFC? We'll do it if you want," Scott said.

"I'm serious about wanting to fight for you guys. I told the UFC I was walking from their offer."

Scott nodded and came back with, "How much do you want?" When I told him $800,000, he didn't hesitate. "Okay, that works for us. And, we'll give you a five-hundred-thousand-dollar signing bonus."

Okay, this works for me too, I thought. Scott made the fighters feel like they were valued and respected, a throwback to working with Pride officials on my contracts. It didn't feel like I was just another sheep in a show. Because of that, I didn't try to leverage the offer with UFC. I accepted the Strikeforce deal.

Dana immediately made disparaging statements to the media. "For the money he wanted, he's not worth it. He's not a big pay-per-view star, he's not a big attraction, and he's not going to sell out arenas. He wants way too much, and he doesn't bring anything to the table."

He said some other shit, and tried to mitigate me signing with Strikeforce, but the reality was, it was only business for him. Some fighters might have taken what he said to heart, but I wasn't offended. I understood that letting go of a star meant you would have to say some fucked-up things about them, especially since it was only about compensation.

My first Strikeforce fight was for the middleweight championship against Jake Shields in April 2010. Jake was the current champion and had been champ for several other organizations in the past. I'm a big fan of country music, and the fight was in Nashville, Tennessee, home of country music. After tweaking my back in training, it had been giving me problems, but I didn't want to pull out. I had a big group of my regulars that were going to the fight along with some country singer friends. *I can't pull out. This is your first fight on national television.* Strikeforce had a deal with CBS, and our fight was broadcast live. Looking back, I should have pulled out.

When I arrived in Nashville on a Monday, I was fifteen pounds over the target weight of 185. I had gotten approved to take medicine for my back, but that *really* fucked with my weight more. Then, night before weigh-ins, I was 205 pounds. I wasn't eating or drinking much, and I nearly killed myself to make weight the next day. Still, I almost finished Jake in the first round. I dropped him a couple times, but then my stamina left me due to the weight cut. He took me down and humped me for three and a half rounds and won a unanimous decision. Jake was a good fighter, but there is no way he would have been able to take me down if my energy wasn't zapped. It was one of those situations where I thought my mental fortitude would be enough to win. Unfortunately, it wasn't.

I wished I had done better, especially with the money I was making, but I couldn't cry about spilled milk. I'm sure there were a handful of people that were rooting against me and glad I had a hiccup, but in war, you may lose a battle, but can trudge forward to win the war.

I took a few months off to let my back heal. My three-fight win streak had been broken, and I was set on not losing two straight fights in Strikeforce. In September, Scott asked me if I would be ready to fight in December, and I told him yes. I had just turned forty but was feeling good after letting my back recover.

In December, I took on Babalu in a rematch of our Rings finale in St. Louis, Missouri. He had been the Strikeforce Light Heavyweight Champion, but we were much different fighters from our 2000 fight. Babalu wanted revenge, but my game plan hadn't changed. I didn't want to grapple with him and knew I could turn out his lights. And that's what happened. In an exchange we ended up on the ground, and I threw my patented punch from the St. Louis Cardinals' bullpen which landed to his face. I saw his eyes roll around and look in different directions. He was still halfway defending, so I threw a few more punches until John McCarthy came in to put a stop to the fight.

After the fight, time started going a little bit faster. I brought in the New Year, which meant my forty-first birthday. I still believed I could beat the best in the world. If I didn't, I probably would've called it quits.

And then I got another shot at a championship belt. After the win, Strikeforce gave me the opportunity to fight for the light heavyweight title in March 2011. I accepted and flew to Columbus, Ohio, to take on the champ, Rafael Cavalcante. I wanted to prove I could still be a world champion—and I did. When you get older, you might lose speed, vision, and timing, but you don't lose power. In the third round, my H-Bomb caught him on the jaw. It sent him face first to the ground, and I got on his back and threw more right hands to his face until the ref came in to stop the fight. Once again, I was one of the best; I had become Strikeforce Light Heavyweight Champion.

I was excited about my win but got goosebumps when I got a call from Scott about my next opponent. "Dan, would you be up for fighting a heavyweight?"

"I'm up for fighting anybody, Scott," I said.

"Great. What about Fedor?"

Fedor Emelianenko was the Mike Tyson or Muhammad Ali of MMA. In Pride, he was finishing the best heavyweights in the world. He had beaten former UFC or Pride champs like Mark Coleman, Frank Mir, Andrei Arlovski, Kevin Randleman, Tim Sylvia, Mark Hunt, and Big Nog. Hell, he even finished Rampage a few years after our fight. He may be the greatest heavyweight mixed martial artist of all time. But I was up for the challenge. This seemed like a Pride matchup, a fight that would be intriguing for people to watch. Two guys in different weight classes who think they are the pound-for-pound best.

We fought July 30, 2011, in Chicago, Illinois. My new girlfriend, Rachel, was one of the multiple people in my entourage that were nervous. I didn't understand why. It was just a fight. Yes, Fedor had finished over 90 percent of his fights, but it wasn't like he was a mutant X-Man. My father and Bob were superheroes, not Fedor.

Even Dana commented before the fight: "If I've got to still give Fedor his digs, my dig would be, 'Dude, you're fighting a 185-pounder.' Henderson's got a great chin, he's durable, he's got good wrestling, he can stay out of submissions, and all the great things I can say about Henderson, but Henderson weighs 185 pounds. So I actually think this fight, as far as Fedor is concerned, it's a lose-lose for him. If he knocks out Dan Henderson, he knocks out a 185-pounder. If he gets knocked out, he just got knocked out by a 185-pounder."

In the first round, his lunchbox mitts dropped me to the ground, but I was more stunned than hurt. He jumped on top of me and tried to finish me, but I was able to sweep him. I threw an uppercut to his chin in our transition and rocked him, then kept punching until Herb Dean pushed me off of him.

After the fight I threw my fight shorts in my gym bag at the lockers and went to the room next door to get stitched up. When I went back to the locker room, I grabbed my bag and didn't think much until I got home. About a week after the fight, I went through my fight bag and saw my shorts missing. Nobody from home had touched my bag, so I was trying to figure out what the fuck happened. I got a call from the Las Vegas Fight Shop who said someone was trying to sell them my Fedor fight trunks. They knew I never sold any of my previous fight shorts, so it raised a red flag with them. I made a social media post detailing my missing gear. A fan direct-messaged me and sent me a picture of a guy who allegedly tried to sell him my shorts. I sent the picture to a Zuffa employee who said the thief was former UFC hype man Burt Watson's nephew, who was working for Zuffa at the time. I called Burt, and he said his nephew had nothing to do with it and denied having a part in it. I even asked Dana to try to track the culprit down, to no avail. To this day I'm still missing those fight shorts.

It was definitely one of the greatest accomplishments of my career, but after the fight I was in limbo. Zuffa had bought Strikeforce in March, but I had hoped Strikeforce would've been able to compete with the UFC, which would have given fighters more options. They had been building momentum, but there were rumors earlier that year that Zuffa would buy them out. Strikeforce had both MMA legends and rising stars; it was only a matter of time until they rivaled the UFC. But that didn't happen. The Fertittas and Dana were smart and put a stop to the Strikeforce machine. Zuffa purchased them in March 2011, which also coincided with the Fedor fight being the last of my contract. As an independent contractor, I didn't know what the fuck was going to happen. I wanted to defend my belt but wasn't sure what Dana and company had in store for me. After all, I was going to have to negotiate with them once again, but this time my number had gone up.

★ ★ ★

14

THE GREATEST FIGHT THAT NEVER WAS

Today, we are in a world where everyone is worrying. Worried about tomorrow, worried about finances, worried about relationships. It doesn't help that there is a diagnosis for almost every fuckin' thing, every single worry. After checking off all the non-worry boxes, people are now worried about not being worried. A big ol' revolving paradox.

I was raised completely opposite, to have no worries about the future. If I did have something to worry about, my dad would be quick to point out he could give me something to worry about—his two-by-fours or wood-frame-molding whip. So, every time there was a crossroads in my career, finding a new sport, new contract, or new promotion, I didn't worry about what was outside of my control. I didn't know what the acquisition of Strikeforce meant for Zuffa, but I must have been too big of a name for them to let me stay in Strikeforce. Hell, they probably even had to pay more for the promotion since I was the champion. And my win over Fedor had made my value go up. If the UFC had paid my asking price before Strikeforce, I probably wouldn't have gotten the deal that I did.

In fact, the new negotiations with the UFC were minimal. I told the media that Dana missed me, that's why they bought Strikeforce, and my manager got a deal done quickly with Dana and Joe Silva. I let bygones be bygones. I'm not sure if they expedited and agreed to terms because of the FTC investigation they were under, but after they purchased Strikeforce, questions were raised about the UFC being a monopoly. If they had fighters who complained about being offered worse contracts following the purchase, it would not have been a good look for them. They needed to show the FTC I was being paid *more*. So, they gave me a raise without question with pay I was happy with.

UFC definitely made the right business decision in buying Strikeforce. They bolstered their roster by bringing over future UFC champs like: Daniel "DC" Cormier, Fabricio Werdum, Tyron Woodley, and Luke Rockhold. A couple years later, they brought over future cash cow Ronda Rousey, who was able to help take mixed martial arts to a wider audience and another level of stardom. Who knows what would have happened if Strikeforce stuck around with the talent they had. Zuffa kept the Strikeforce brand until January 2013 when they officially dissolved the promotion but brought me right back into the UFC without a defense of my title. I guess I was valuable to them since they wasted no time in my third stint with them.

They scheduled me for a main-event fight on November 19, 2011, four months after my TKO over Fedor. I would be facing someone new, another Pride veteran, Shogun Rua. Ironically, the UFC had booked my fight ten years to almost the day I had beaten his brother, Ninja. I knew he would be tougher. Shogun's career had simply outshined Ninja's. He had finished guys like Rampage, Alistair Overeem twice, Chuck Liddell, Forrest Griffin, Lyoto Machida, Little Nog, Mark Coleman, and Kevin Randleman. Besides that, he had youth on his side. He was thirty and in his prime while I had just celebrated my forty-first birthday.

The fight was an absolute fuckin' war. A blind person could tell it was a bloodfest with the commentary by Joe Rogan and Mike

Goldberg. Before it was even over, Joe and Mike were calling it one of the greatest fights of all time.

I may have underestimated Shogun's heart a bit. I cut his eye in the first exchange and had him hurt. I thought about unloading everything I had, but with it being a five-round fight, I didn't want to exhaust myself and come up short. I hurt him again in the second round, but it seemed like every time that happened, he wouldn't cave. The third round was different. I hit him again in the eye with a winding H-Bomb that crumpled him. I thought to myself, *For sure he's done.* I jumped on him and threw punches to his head, waiting for the ref to stop it, but the ref didn't come in. Shogun was able to turtle up and avoid some of my bigger shots. *Fuck.* The next two rounds I was fuckin' spent. My white shorts looked like they'd been dipped in blood. You couldn't even read the sponsors on them anymore. I went on autopilot, and Shogun handily beat me in Round Five. He even got the mount several times but was too tired to do shit. His punches didn't hurt me. I felt perfectly fine.

There was nervous anticipation about the decision from others. A lot of people thought it was a close fight, but I didn't think so. I had clearly won the first three rounds, the fourth round could have gone either way, and even though my face looked like I had been in a fight, Shogun's looked like he had been mugged. In the moment, I didn't know the gravity or significance of the battle we had until I watched it back. Everyone was clamoring about it, and when I watched it over, I understood the hoopla around it, but I was never in danger the entire fight. He needed to finish me to win the fight.

We both didn't want to lose the fight; neither of us had wanted to give up an inch. I still can't believe Shogun was able to withstand my assault. I hit him with everything I had, and he was able to go the distance. Although I won the fight, he earned much more respect from me.

In May 2018 the UFC inducted our fight at UFC 139 into their Hall of Fame. I had no idea they were going to do that until I got a call to attend the ceremony. I thought it was cool because I didn't know the UFC inducted individual fights into their ring of honor. More importantly, I was glad to have put on a show that night in San Jose, California. The fans were the real winners, and the UFC has called it "The Fight of the Century." Even Dana said, "This fight is one of the top three fights of all time." When the media asked him what were the other two, he didn't know.

Following the fight, I knew my stock was on the rise again. I was like the stock market; I had mostly bull runs and some bear markets in my career, but fans always wanted to tune in to see the outcome. They knew I would bring it.

Dana, always the businessman, asked me what I wanted to do next. Me being back on the UFC roster and putting on a performance like that, I was back in the driver's seat. I told him I wanted another title shot.

Jon "Bones" Jones was the 205-pound title holder and a young phenom who had shot up to stardom quickly. He was the youngest champion in UFC history, and I wanted to test my mettle against his. For some reason, he was untouchable to the guys he was fighting, but I thought my style matched up well with his.

Dana said, "I promised Rashad (Evans) a title shot against Jon if he wins his fight in January. You can fight the winner if you want to wait that long."

I wanted to fight the best, so I was willing to wait it out. I would have gotten paid the same show money to fight some Joe Blow, but that's not why I was in the sport.

Rashad did get his title shot against Jon in April 2012 but ended up losing a not-so-close decision. They were former training partners, and I knew Rashad's style didn't match up well against Jon. After the fight, Dana announced to the media that I would fight Jon next. I was going to be forty-two and getting another shot at a world championship.

The fight was set as the main event on September 1, 2012, at UFC 151 in Vegas. The media and fight fans were intrigued by Jon and his calm demeanor. Was there a fighting style that the young champ would struggle with? He hadn't been hit hard, he did a great job of imposing his will and game plan on others, but I thought my strengths and skills were better than his and was excited to show it.

I had five months to prepare for Jon's style, and training camp was going great. I felt like I was twenty-six again and in the best shape of my life. I knew Jon was long, but he didn't have KO power like I did. My plan was to utilize kicks to clinch with him, then dirty box, clinch and follow up with more kicks. I figured those would set up my power punches and combinations. I had sparred with guys his size and was ready to fight someone that long. None of the former champs he had beaten, Shogun, Rampage, or Lyoto Machida, had the same wrestling prowess or power that I had.

Unfortunately, it never happened. Three weeks before the fight, I was training with my teammate, Rameau Sokoudjou, when my battle plans for Jon came crashing down. Sokoudjou, a master judo practitioner and tough fighter, shifted his weight quickly on my knee, and my MCL popped. I knew it was bad right away. It wasn't his fault, though. Sokoudjou is just so damn explosive. He's accidentally hurt more ankles and knees in my gym than anyone else. It was just his style. In all my years of training with him, it had never happened to me.

I went to my athletic trainers and physical therapists, and they confirmed the MCL tear. What made it even more devastating was the tear in the ligament was worse than my first one against Big Nog. I had never pulled out of a fight in fifteen years of fighting, and I did everything I could to avoid it. I stopped training and stuck to cardio with weights. After a week, it still felt loose and sore. A week before the fight, I practiced to see if I could make it, but my coaches told me I needed to call it off. I didn't want to, but I knew they had my best interest in mind.

I finally called Dana to let him know the situation, and he wanted me to get checked by their doctors, which was standard practice. He flew me to Vegas for an MRI, and they confirmed that it was a bad tear. I would've been useless in the cage. Dana made the announcement that I pulled out of the fight, and he asked Chael Sonnen to step in. Chael agreed to fight Jon, but the card got cancelled. Jon refused to fight Chael because he thought the situation was a conspiracy. I'm not sure what the big deal was. There is no way I would fake an injury. I've seen other guys cry wolf for a win or opt out of fighting, but I think I would've hurt Jon pretty bad. And if he was in shape to fight me—why not fight Chael right away?

The UFC ended up scrapping the whole UFC 151 card, the first time a PPV was canceled in UFC history. Jon submitted Vitor three weeks later at UFC 152, and it took me over a year to heal from my injury. It was the greatest fight that never happened because Jon was the real deal.

This made 2012 the first and only year in my career I didn't have a fight. It gave me an opportunity to hang out with my kids, who were getting to be in their teens, and figure out some of my personal life, and grow closer to my girlfriend. I didn't have marriage plans, I vowed to never do it again, but she made me happy.

When my MCL finally healed, the UFC wanted me to face former champ Lyoto Machida. I had first seen Lyoto fight in the World Fighting Alliance in 2006 and thought he was boring as shit. I told them it wasn't going to be fan friendly. "All he's going to do is run." But that's what they wanted since Chael did a good job in finally talking himself into a fight with Jon.

The UFC put me and Lyoto on the co-main event at UFC 157 in February 2013. The only reason we weren't the headliners, was because for the first time in UFC history, women would fight in the UFC, so there was a giant buildup. Ronda Rousey was fighting Liz Carmouche, and the winner would be the first female UFC champ.

Dana had been getting some backlash for saying women would "never" fight in the UFC but had since done a 180. Women were good for business. I had been around women wrestling and had no problem with them fighting. I knew women's MMA wasn't close to the skill caliber of men's at that time, but now you see women like Amanda Nunes and Valentina Shevchenko who are well-rounded. Just like the men, they needed to evolve—and have.

About a month before my fight, I threw a body kick, but it was blocked by an elbow. After that, my ankle felt like shit, and it started to affect my training, so I asked for a cortisone shot to help my slight limp. Before administering the shot, the doctors did an X-ray on my ankle and asked, "How long has it been broken?" I didn't know what they were talking about. *There's no way it could be fuckin' broken.* A minute later they pointed to the X-ray and said, "There's an older break a couple inches higher." I was confused. "I had no idea I had broke it before, Doc," I said.

I wasn't about to pull out of another fight. The pain was bearable, so I could still fight. What I wasn't going to do was baby my injury. Go 100 percent or don't go at all.

The fight with Machida was more like a fifteen-minute cross-country run. I should've trained on the track the whole time. That is all he did. He would throw one or two strikes, then run. I would chase him down, then he would do the same. He didn't want to engage at all.

Randy's last fight of his career was unfortunately a knockout loss to Machida, but I couldn't get the guy to fight me at all. When time expired, I thought, *There's no way this motherfucker wins this.* But when the decision was read, I was shocked and dead wrong. The judges gave him a split-decision win, which baffles me to this day. What was fucked up about it even more was the fact that they wouldn't let me get a crack at Jon.

A month later I was at Bellator 92 in Temecula, California, to corner a fighter from my gym, and the judges in the back were talking about the outcome of my fight with Machida. They were pissed off at the two judges who scored it against me. They said those judges had no criteria for giving Machida the win.

It was good reaffirmation of how I thought it should have been scored but little solace. I wasn't going to get a title shot coming off a loss.

In June 2013, I was booked as the headliner for UFC 161 against another former champ, Rashad Evans. It wasn't a fight to write home about, he had had the light heavyweight belt for one fight, but was knocked out by Machida and couldn't get by Jon. The fight was made to see where we were both at.

I thought the outcome was quite clear. Rashad couldn't handle my power; I had stuck him with a sharp jab that sent him on skates. Yes, he recovered, but just tried to take me down about ten times. I was a little winded in the third but had done far more damage.

That's not how two of the judges saw it. Bruce Buffer announced Rashad as the winner by split decision. Even Rashad was surprised he won. He gave a little laugh when Joe Rogan interviewed him and said, "I don't know who was hitting. I thought the ref was kicking me or something. I don't know what happened. I was asking my corner 'What hit me, what hit me, what hit me?' They said, 'He caught you with a punch.' I said, 'No shit.'"

It was like the Olympics all over again. Two split-decision losses in a row. I couldn't catch a break. It sucks even more when your opponent thinks they lost as well. In Pride, those would have been two wins for me, and I would've probably gotten a title shot. Instead, they booked a rematch with Vitor in Brazil, a fight I wasn't motivated for.

This was another one of those fights where I had nothing to gain. Vitor had lost his title fight against Jon, but with two straight losses, I had little say. And Vitor looked to be back on a buffet of steroids. His previous two fights had been in Brazil, and at thirty-six, his body looked like Mr. Olympia. There's only one way a body transformation happens that fast. And with the fight in Brazil, no one cared about drug tests.

In the first minute of the fight, I got caught with a left uppercut as I was throwing my own punches and fell to the canvas. Vitor jumped on me as the Brazilian fans were screaming wildly. I was still coherent as he was throwing punches with his Hulk-sized arms. It was when I tried to get up, he caught me with a head kick that dropped me back down. The kick stunned me, I was still aware of what was going on, but the ref didn't give me a chance to defend. He waved the fight off, and it went in the record books as a KO. I wish they would've let it go a little bit longer. I knew what was going on and, with my experience, could have recovered. I could see if I wasn't aware of my surroundings, but it wasn't meant to be. The loss put me on a three-fight losing streak for the first time in my career, and thoughts of retirement fluttered in my head.

☆☆☆
15

COMING TO A CLOSE?

The fight with Vitor was the last on my contract. Two years earlier I was the hammer, now I was the nail. Every previous UFC fight of mine had been on PPV, but the Vitor rematch was on cable television. During contract negotiations, I took a decent pay cut to stay with the UFC, but after briefly flirting with retirement in my head, at forty-three, I knew I still had gas left in the tank. I wanted to spend more time with my family, and my body wasn't recovering from practices as quickly. I was spending too much time on the couch. I was like the old boxer who knew they could still win given the right opportunity. After my loss, I took a few weeks off, and that's when I got a call from the UFC for another rematch.

"We want you to fight Shogun again. The fans want to see it."

I could see why the fans wanted the fight, but it wasn't a fight that excited me. I wanted to fight the champ or, at least, someone that got me closer to the belt. Shogun had gone 2–2 since our epic war, and his stock wasn't raising any eyebrows, but neither was mine, so I took the fight, and they sent me to Brazil for our sequel.

There are positives and negatives to every decision you make. If you prepare for something new—a job, date, or activity—you might put a bit more effort into it. I wasn't preparing for someone new (negative), but the twenty-five minutes I spent in the cage helped me prepare better. It seemed like I was always getting the best version of people every time I fought them. I had to get ready for the best Shogun. This time, I wouldn't underestimate his heart.

The fight was in Natal, Brazil, a beautiful city, but the arena was a tropical oven. It was ninety-four degrees inside with 86 percent humidity. It was muggy as fuck. I was a 2–1 underdog, and as soon as the fight started, the Brazilians started with their usual chant, "Uh vai morrer," or, "You're going to die."

Even though I was prepared to fight for five rounds, I'm glad it didn't go a second longer. Towards the end of the first round, I caught him with a punch that briefly dropped him, and I moved forward for the kill. I had Shogun against the fence and threw some punches and knees when—*fwack!* Shogun threw a left hook from hell, and my legs looked like a newborn calf's. I stumbled down, and Shogun started throwing flaming hooks that were finding a home on my face. *Where the fuck am I at?* I was seriously hurt. I grabbed the fence and tried to get up, but Shogun was able to pull me down right away. I ate an elbow and some more punches until the round ended.

I waddled back to my corner, and they put a large ice bag over my head. I didn't hear a word my corner said. I knew I still needed to recover. In the second round, I decided not to push forward like I normally did, but it didn't help. Shogun marched towards me and caught me with some huge overhand rights. I was able to exchange punches with him, but then I shot for a takedown from way too far away. *I'm fighting, right?* I was seeing both stars and cobwebs. Then, halfway through the round, Shogun threw an uppercut that crumpled me and knocked the cobwebs away. It was only stars floating around.

That might have been the best thing for me. Shogun wasn't able to mount additional offense, and I was able to take those couple minutes to recover. *I'm going to need these last three rounds and need to get my ass moving,* I thought.

In the third round, I felt fully recovered and went on the offense again. I was finally able to land my big right hand. We clinched briefly but the humidity was going to make it difficult for me to take Shogun down. I pushed him off, and as I did, threw a Mike Tyson-esque punch that sent him rolling twenty feet back. I rushed in for the finish and threw some more punches and hammer fists. Shogun had one arm around my leg but was lifeless. Herb Dean said, "Fight back, fight back," but he didn't move. That was enough for Herb to call the fight, and when we unclasped, Shogun collapsed back like he had just been shot. His nose looked like it was next to his ear.

The crowd went dead silent. It took Shogun a couple minutes to come to, but I had the utmost respect for him and went over to help him up. In the post-fight interview, I thanked him for the battles and told him I was a fan of his. Our rematch, like the first, went down as one of the greatest fights ever. I saw Herb at the hotel bar after the fight, and he told me, "You know, I was a second away from calling the fight in the first. You were hurt bad." I thanked him for not stopping the fight but didn't realize how hurt I was until I watched it back.

I was glad to get a win after nearly three years, and I stayed in Natal a few days with friends and family. The Brazilians were nice everywhere I went. They get pumped for their fighters, so there was never hard feelings when they chant for me "to die." It was all respect with them outside of the arena.

There was some satisfaction in knowing I still could win by knockout. My self-belief had never wavered, but even split-decision losses will make media, fans, and the promotion doubt you. The highlight-reel knockout made everyone take notice once again.

The next day, Dana called and asked me to fight Daniel Cormier at UFC 173 in May 2014. That gave me only seven weeks to prepare, but the UFC had issues putting the card together and knew they could depend on me. Vitor was one of the reasons. He was next in line for a title shot against Chris Weidman, but didn't want to get drug tested in Vegas, so the fight was pulled.

I had bought an International Scout as a 4x4 project, and even though I was training 100 percent for DC, I would head over to my buddy's body shop to work on it every day. I wanted to be able to get it up and running to see what it could do off-roading, and my interests in fighting were slowly waning. I wasn't slacking during practice or complacent; my brain needed additional stimulation, and I thought it was healthy to have distractions from the next fight.

Fight week for UFC 173 was much different than before. It was the first time the UFC was filming their *Embedded* series. A camera crew followed me the whole week, and it was able to get my interactions with DC.

DC was a fantastic freestyle wrestler and former 2004 Olympian who had competed at 211 pounds. I followed his career at Strikeforce, where he won the heavyweight title, and had been a fan of his ever since. The respect went both ways. In the lead-up to the fight, he said, "Dan Henderson is the model for what I want to be in the sport."

I knew he was much bigger than me and was dropping massive weight to get to 206 pounds, the maximum at which he could officially fight at 205 in a non-title fight. If this was a title fight, there would be no one-pound excess weight allowance. Popeyes was his favorite chicken, so I bought some and brought it down to the workout room while he was there. I was hoping he would have a tougher weight cut if he consumed the chicken. He didn't.

DC was a 10–1 favorite going into the fight, and we both had aspirations of fighting Jon for the title. I liked the guy and always rooted for him in his fights, but this was one fight I wanted him to lose. The day of the fight, DC weighed a whopping 228 pounds, and I came in at a paltry 199. The thirty-pound difference didn't worry me; I knew he would use his weight efficiently, but he used it better than I thought. I found that out quickly in the first round when he was on top of me in side control. It felt like a ton of bricks was on me.

DC's wrestling acumen had taught him how to use his weight. I knew he didn't want to strike with me, but I thought I would be able to defend his takedowns better. By the third round, I was worn out. The crowd gasped when he picked me up and slammed me, but it didn't hurt. I was simply fatigued. It was an ode to my wrestling days. I would never randomly wrestle someone two weight classes heavier. This was the style that was difficult; if all things are equal, the bigger man is going to win. With just over a minute left in the fight, DC was able to take my back and lock in a rear naked choke. I tried to roll out of it, but it didn't work. I got choked unconscious.

After the fight, Joe Rogan said, "Dan never tapped. There's not a tougher man that's ever walked the face of the planet than Dan Henderson."

In the post-fight interview, I was appreciative of the fans and acknowledged that DC was the better man that night. He went on to do great things in the UFC, including becoming a double champ like me. I knew I'd have to get back in line for a title shot, and after the fight, I said to myself, *I'm going back to 185 because these fuckers are too heavy.*

☆☆☆
1 6

BAD BLOOD | TIME TO SAY GOODBYE

The fight adage "knowing when it's time to hang it up," will never grow old. Fighters will age, athletes decline, but the sport will always be there. I was honest with myself. At forty-four, I was no longer in my prime, but I could still compete at the highest level.

And it wasn't because my skills were deteriorating, but my body needed more time to recover. I'm not sure when that changed, but I didn't want to miss my kids growing up either. Three months after my fight with DC, I surprised my girlfriend, Rachel, at my annual pig roast by asking her to marry me. After she said yes, I told her and all the attendees that we would be getting married in thirty minutes since we had all our family and friends there. I already had a cake, and had my neighbor ordained to marry us.

After my divorce, I didn't think I would marry again, but Rachel and I just clicked. I wanted to be sure that I wouldn't have to go through it again. We had been together for three years and built a trust. I wouldn't have gotten married again if I thought I'd have to go through another ugly divorce.

———————

I got back into the cage for a co-main event fight in January 2015. I've had some bad stoppages and outcomes in my mixed martial arts career, but this was probably the worst stoppage of them all. I had been robbed of wins by judges, but this time, it wasn't because of them.

My next fight was against Gegard Mousasi, who was ranked in the top ten of the division. I had trained with Mousasi a few times at my gym. He had been passing through Southern California a few years before, and wanted to get some different training in. I was able to spar and grapple with him and was able to get enough information in those sessions to be confident going into the fight. Plus, he had a style that I was used to.

The fight was booked in Stockholm, Sweden, and it brought back memories of wrestling there when we made intermittent trips from the Soviet Union. But I didn't have time to see old wrestling buddies. I wanted to take care of business and get back home.

The fight with Mousasi didn't go long. He threw a punch that grazed and slit my eyelid, and I thought, *Oh shit!* When I had cornered Randy in his fight against Vitor, the same thing happened to him. One of Randy's eyelids was also slit, and he had to get it patched after the fight. After I felt my eye was fucked up, I didn't want the ref or doctor stopping the fight, so I went after him. With just over a minute in the fight, I ducked my head and threw a right hand, but Mousasi threw his own right, which grazed the top of my head. I slipped and fell, but when I turned to get up, my feet weren't planted, and he brushed me with a jab as my momentum brought me back.

It didn't help when I rolled my ass back and the back of my head hit the fence. I had no idea I was that close to the fence. I knew judges saw that shit as a negative. It can be the aesthetics for them; they may think it was worse than it is. To mitigate that, I leaned my head forward and grabbed Mousasi's leg for a takedown of my own. But I couldn't finish it. The incompetent ref grabbed me from behind and waved the fight off.

"What the fuck are you doing? Are you fuckin' kidding me?" I was pissed. I'm usually laid back, but I couldn't comprehend how this new ref just stopped my livelihood. This was my place of work, and I was both angry and flummoxed.

"I know, I'm sorry," was all that he told me.

You can watch the broadcast back and see our exchange. Mousasi wasn't too happy with the stoppage either. But it wasn't his fault. The beauty of mixed martial arts is just because you get knocked down, it doesn't mean the fight is over. Let a fighter properly finish their opponent.

Social media had mixed reactions to the outcome. Some thought my career was done with the stoppage warranted, while others agreed it was too quick. Dana tweeted, "If the ref didn't tackle Mousasi he would have kept that top position Dan would have got smashed." But Dana had never fought in a cage.

After the fight my eye had a weird feeling. The eyelid was slit open, but it didn't hurt. I told the doctors, so we stayed in Stockholm a couple extra days for a specialist to stitch it up. Rachel thought it was funny I was going to have to wear an eye patch, so she drew an eyeball on it before they stitched me up. I had gotten fucked, but at least I had my new bride by my side.

You know, if you keep running, you'll eventually get there. I felt like I had been running the professional combat sports route for years. I could tell I was going to get there, I just didn't know where "there" was. There were murmurs from the media and fans that I should've retired after the Mousasi fight. But there were some who said that after the DC fight and my previous losses as well. The more time went by, the more I heard the terms "pioneer" and "legend." My next fight might have shocked many of the cynics, but not me.

In my post-fight interview with UFC commentator Jon Anik, he said, "One of the greatest mixed martial artists to ever live, Dan Henderson, adds yet another chapter to his legacy here tonight. A lot of naysayers coming into this one, you muted all of them, congratulations, how are you feeling about your performance?"

I finished Tim "The Barbarian" Boetsch in twenty-eight seconds with the magical H-Bomb in New Orleans, Louisiana, on June 6, 2015. Tim was ranked in the top fifteen of the division, and I had dismantled him quickly. The right hand was still there. I felt strong going into the fight, but in the post-fight interview, when I heard "one of the greatest," I knew my clock was ticking quicker. It might have been a good win to go out on, but I wasn't quite ready to let go.

I didn't want to retire prematurely, but I didn't want to hang on too long either. It was like my wrestling career. I needed to have an exit strategy and know when it was the right time. I had had mixed martial arts to get into, but after MMA, what was next?

The UFC booked a rubber match with me and Vitor in November. I didn't understand the matchup and wasn't sure what the fight was going to determine. Every time I had fought him, he looked to be on some type of banned substance, and there was a pattern to his highlight wins. In his last few fights, he had finished Bisping, Rockhold, and Anthony Johnson, all fights in Brazil, and lost to Jon Jones and Chris Weidman, both fights in North America. Our fight was scheduled for November in a city I was somewhat familiar with, São Paulo, Brazil.

In October 2015, the UFC finally implemented USADA. The drug testing was about to get tougher. But USADA didn't have oversight in Brazil. All they could do was work with doctors and commissions there. For my fight with Vitor, I was told his doctor was also the head of the athletic commission in Brazil. Even though I was clean, I would still have to deal with a juiced-up Vitor. It's fascinating how his body can go from flabby in the States to bulked up in two to three months.

The fight went similarly to our previous bout. Vitor threw a left high kick that rocked me. I dropped down from some punches and was defending, then the ref put a halt to the match. I had been hurt far worse in the Shogun fight, but Herb Dean wasn't the ref against Vitor. I couldn't control the stoppage.

Some people ask me, "Why did you fight him if you knew he was on steroids?" The truth is, whenever I went into a fight, I never thought twice about it. I thought I could beat anyone, steroids or not. I wasn't one to dwell on something, even after they got caught. I do think there should be a disclaimer on everyone's record who got caught cheating. I'm not sure if you should put an asterisk, star, or underline, but it definitely should be noted.

In January 2016, the UFC called me for another rematch. They wanted me to face Machida in April. Our first fight had been a snooze fest. I didn't think anything was going to change. I let Dana know what I thought, but he still wanted to make it happen. I took the fight, but this time I didn't have a fucked-up ankle and I was preparing for a fight on wheels.

I flew into Tampa for our April 16 fight, but it came to a screeching halt. Dana scrapped the fight two days before weigh-ins when Machida tested positive for PEDs. I asked Dana if I would get my show money since I was ready to fight. Dana would pay fighters that money most of the time. But not for me. He gave me between $20,000–$25,000, which wasn't close to my fight purse. The money barely covered training camp. My fifty loyal friends and family that flew to Florida for the fight didn't get a dime back. I still think Machida should pay me money for that fight. If you are caught using banned substances, that fighter should be liable for their opponents' wages.

When I got back to California, I knew my retirement clock was ticking. I wasn't going to wait for Machida to serve his suspension, so the UFC matched me against a former Cuban Olympic judoka, Héctor Lombard.

I was familiar with Héctor after he had come to my gym a few years prior to train. He contacted me through a mutual friend, and I welcomed him in. He was a strong, talented fighter, but whenever I left town, there would be issues with him. I would get messages from people saying he was trying to knock out his training partners while warming up or drilling in my gym. He never tried his antics while I was there; I was waiting for him to do something so I could put him in his place. The goal of training is to make yourself and teammates better, not use them as punching bags to feed your ego.

Héctor eventually left my gym on his own accord. No one liked him, but it wasn't personal. And I had never had bad blood or a genuine animosity for another fighter, but apparently Héctor felt unwelcome and took it to heart. He talked shit right after the fight was booked. "He never gave a fuck about me. I went there and he never talked to me, so I was like, okay, no worries...I'm going to go and knock him out."

Nothing he said bothered me. At our pre-fight face-offs, he tried to get in my head and asked, "Who said I was bullying them?" Instead of pulling me aside to talk to me, he did it in front of the cameras. Did he think that was smart? He had gotten busted for an anabolic steroid the year before, so maybe his gym antics were 'roid rage. And he was trying to save face for the cameras.

On June 4, 2016, I entered the cage at UFC 199 at The Forum in Inglewood, California, for what I thought could be my last fight. I was inching towards forty-six, and I wasn't sure how my story was going to end. I wanted to knock Héctor out; beyond that I had no idea.

When the fight started, I could hear the chants start. "U-S-A! U-S-A!" I got chills hearing this. I knew I needed to perform. And Héctor was much more dangerous than Machida. He had heavy hands and would come to fight.

"Let's go Hendo! Let's go Hendo!" The crowd continued with their chants. Me and Héctor started to exchange back-and-forth punches. I dropped him, then he dropped me halfway through the first round. After we got back to our feet, Héctor threw a Cuban missile left hook that sent me headfirst towards the canvas. It was a good thing Herb Dean was reffing, because he gave me time to defend.

After I was able to get back up, Héctor started throwing 100 mph fastballs once again. He clipped me with a punch, and I grabbed him, and he judo threw me to the ground. Then-UFC-commentator Mike Goldberg said on the broadcast, "Hendo close to being finished." I looked a little dazed, but my head was still there. But even Joe Rogan questioned me. "But after all these wars he's had inside the Octagon and outside the Octagon in other organizations, you got to wonder how much is left of that chin. The power is still there."

After I made it to the second round, Joe said, "You can't quantify the kind of mental toughness Dan Henderson has. The ability to ride out storms." I had recovered when the second round started. The pace slowed down, and Héctor seemed content just standing right in front of me. I tried to time my H-Bomb, but I didn't get a chance to. After a few feints, I threw a high right head kick to his dome. Héctor grabbed my leg, but a millisecond later I cocked my right hand forward and unleashed a vicious backward elbow that connected with his temple. He dropped like a sack of potatoes. I followed with a nasty elbow and, as Herb came in to stop the fight, wound up for one more elbow.

When I got up, sixteen thousand fans had exploded into cheers. Joe said, "Oh my goodness. Dan Henderson is an animal. That guy is an animal. Wow." Héctor was out cold. I turned his lights out, eyes closed, good night. The bad blood was gone. I was ready to be done.

After everyone cleared out of the cage, I had my children hop in to take pictures with me. I wanted them to remember my last fight. It was the last fight on my contract, and I wasn't going to do a multi-fight extension. But a week after the fight, Dana called.

"What do you think about fighting Bisping?" Bisping had just won the middleweight title on the same card as me. He had a highlight knockout over Luke Rockhold, and I guess they thought a rematch made sense. "It would be for the belt," Dana said. "And you can retire win or lose."

A title fight was the only thing that made sense to me. I was ranked twelfth in the middleweight division and, under normal circumstances, wouldn't have gotten the opportunity. "I'll do it," I said. "I'm done after this, though."

It was bittersweet knowing that I had made my decision to retire after my rematch with Bisping. I would have been fine riding out into the sunset with the KO over Héctor, but Dana knew he could squeeze one more fight out of me with a title fight.

A month after my forty-sixth birthday, I headed to Manchester, England, for my final fight against Bisping. He was on his high horse talking shit about my age, and he guaranteed a victory. None of it bothered me. I was happy for him. He had come back from adversity. A bulked-up Vitor had kicked and punched Bisping's right eye, which led to a retinal detachment. Bisping eventually lost the eye but continued his career. He was furious about Vitor being on 'roids, which he thought gave him an unfair advantage and a heinous victory, which he probably had every right to, but he could still be a prick.

I had been at UFC 167 in Vegas watching GSP against Johny Hendricks, when Mark Coleman came to sit next to me. My seat was behind Bisping's, and the two of them talked between one of the rounds about Bisping's eye injury. Bisping told Mark how it was difficult for him to see out of it. A few minutes went by, and in the middle of the final round, Mark, who was a little inebriated, tried to get Bisping's attention. "Hey, One-Eyed Bisping! Hey, Bisping. Hey, One-Eyed Bisping."

Bisping finally turned around, visibly upset. "What the fuck is wrong with you? I just talked to you and showed you respect. We can go to the parking lot and I'll beat your ass."

Mark looked surprised. His intent was not to be disrespectful. He contended, "I wasn't trying to fuck with you. You said you could only see out of one eye, so it was a nickname. What's the big deal? I'm an old man. Of course you'll beat my ass."

Bisping didn't back down and was mad-dogging Mark. I finally said, "Hey, relax."

But he wasn't having it. "Fuck you, Hendo, I'll take you out to the parking lot too."

I didn't say anything back. I just chuckled and heard some of the fans around laughing at him too. He might have been slightly inebriated as well. He finally turned around and left the area.

Our fight at UFC 204 started around 4:00 a.m. local time in Manchester, but there wasn't an empty seat at the sold-out Manchester Arena. They wanted to see their local boy, Bisping, defend his new belt. I was there to retire with the one belt that had eluded me, the UFC title.

Bisping surprised me with his fight style. In the first round, he came forward. I wasn't expecting that, but I made him pay the price with a monster right hand that sent him to the floor. I thought the fight was over. I was punching and elbowing him with everything but the kitchen sink, and a sea of blood squirted out of his eye. *This motherfucker is hurt bad.* I threw a couple more punches, but miraculously, he got up. In the second round, I connected again and sent him to the ground. And again I couldn't finish him. The fight went to the judges' scorecards in his hometown.

Two of the judges scored it 48–47 and the other 49–46. I lost the decision. There were no 10–8 rounds awarded to me after almost finishing him in the first two rounds. I was disappointed as fuck. I won't talk about how the Pride judges would've scored it. All you had to do was take a look at our faces. His face was marred with bruises and cuts, and I was fresh. This fight could've taken place on a playground, in a gym, or on the street, and the crowd would've known who won. But alas, I wouldn't get the UFC belt around my waist.

I did give Bisping his credit, but it did leave a sour taste in my mouth. I had worked extremely hard for that fight, and I left everything I had in the cage. As a fighter, I have a level of respect for others who have bled in the ring or cage, but sometimes that's not always reciprocated.

When I was cornering Sam Alvey at a UFC event in 2022, Bisping, who retired in 2017, was one of the commentators. At a Vegas hotel, Bisping walked by an elevator to say hi to Sam when my back was turned, and when I turned around, he'd already walked off. Sam and another coach thought that was weird. "How come he didn't acknowledge you?" I didn't know, but maybe he's still that same guy. There's a reason why there are some fighters who are fan favorites. At least he defended the belt for one fight.

17

THE ART OF WAR | FIGHT AFTER THE FIGHT

Go enroll in a college philosophy course, and you're likely to get one of the professors to pose a question like, "Are we even real, or is life fake and a simulation?" It'll probably have the heads of underclassmen spinning, and fuck their heads up more in this technological, social media world.

They're all full of shit. I know the spacetime continuum exists, because when I look back at where I started, I'm like, *Fuck, how did I get here so fast?*

One day I'm in my dad's non-emission-passing Ford Econoline headed to wrestling practice with Bob Anderson, the next I'm in the second half of my life and getting a little older every day.

And since I retired in 2016, mixed martial arts has grown rapidly. In the seven years I've been retired, the sport has continued to grow at a rapid pace. Today, it is the fastest-growing sport in the world, with the UFC being the premiere show in North America and internationally.

When I got started in 1997, no one had an idea of how much it could skyrocket. But I never put a cap on the growth of the sport. There's always been a naturalness and mystery to it. Hand-to-hand combat has been around since the beginning of mankind, and you never know what could happen when two people face off. That's why there's a high entertainment value to MMA. It just needed two things to scale: more people watching and time.

None of it would have happened if it wasn't for the fighters from the beginning. It's impossible to name them all, but the guys that made the biggest impact are: Royce Gracie, Randy Couture, Don Frye, Ken Shamrock, Bas Rutten, Frank Shamrock, Chuck Liddell, Tito Ortiz, Pat Miletich, Maurice Smith, Sakuraba, Big Nog, Wanderlei, Fedor Emelianenko, Kevin Randleman, Anderson Silva, Rampage, Shogun, Jens Pulver, B. J. Penn, Mark Coleman, Murilo Bustamante, and Mirko Cro Cop. There are many others that have paved the way for the fighters of today that I didn't name.

I appreciate what the promotions have done for the fighters, but there should be so much more done. The Fertittas and Dana did an excellent job in helping MMA grow, but it required fighters to put their blood, sweat, and tears on the line. Zuffa took the UFC from a $2-million gamble to a $4-billion enterprise when they sold it to WME. Dana has been one of the main beneficiaries from his time and effort, but I don't see why he couldn't take 10 or 15 percent of his $300-million-plus profit and cut a check to those early pioneers. It would've shown some gratitude, but he's a business guy, and Dana has Dana's best interests in mind.

Even when fighters were making some supplemental money from sponsors, the UFC took those funds. First they started charging companies to sponsor fighters, which took the monies to about half. Then, when the Reebok deal came along, I lost another $10,000 per fight. I was an independent contractor that wasn't able to work independently. I had to wear Reebok gear for my last couple of fights, and now they have a deal with Venom. (Although for my first event with Reebok, I did tell the Reebok rep I wasn't going to wear their shoes, and I didn't.)

There are still some fighters making $10,000 or $12,000 a fight in the UFC. I don't get how this is possible. There's no way a fighter should be getting that little show money when the promotion is making a shitload of money. I've always understood that it took money to build the machine, but that machine requires fighters. That is not a slight of Dana; I knew their business model early on and appreciate the contributions Dana has made to the sport. When I saw Dana wear a Rage Against the Machine T-shirt, I thought it was ironic. The UFC *is* the machine.

After fighters' careers are over, they usually get put to the wayside. I would've loved to be an ambassador for the sport, but I retired as WME was taking over. I thought I might have been used to help promote the sport, but that was it for me. I was on my own after a career that started with the promotion at UFC 17.

At minimum, there should be a retirement plan and health insurance for fighters through each promotion, or they should have a governing body for a fighters' union. These things would be extremely helpful for guys like me who put in decades of work and a shitload of fights. Also, there are some guys who are suffering the effects of head trauma from the punches and kicks over the years. The NFL has started to address CTE and protect their athletes, but there's nothing for fighters. I'm not sure what all the symptoms of CTE are, but I don't think I've suffered from the blows. I didn't wear headgear in practice or training, it never felt comfortable, but I don't worry about CTE either. For those fighters that may be punch drunk, they should be able to get proper care and help.

I have no complaints about what I did or didn't do; I was able to make my living from the sport. Still, there are many people who recognize me, although none of the younger generation knows who I am. I was surprised during COVID when I had a mask on and people would stop me for pictures or autographs. I would think, *How the hell do these people know who I am?*

I didn't get into fighting to be known or famous. I did it for the competition. I did miss out on two of my life goals: becoming an Olympic gold medalist and winning a UFC belt. It's easy to say now, if I was wrestling on the national team, then I would've gotten into MMA a lot younger. But my wrestling and MMA career were in two different eras. Even the way fighters warm up today before a fight is different. They hit mitts and do light grappling, but when I warmed up, it was intense. My training partner wouldn't go 100 percent on me, but I was basically beating them up a little bit before my fight. I wanted to make sure I would react correctly and get my timing down. This new generation gets a light sweat in before they make the walkout, but I would be mimicking a real fight for forty-five minutes before I headed to the cage. It just seems like a softer generation.

I really would've liked to fight Jon Jones. We did a grappling match in 2016, but I wanted to see how I matched up against him in a fight. After I retired, I never got the itch to come back. I don't watch too many fights, but when I do, sometimes I think about how I would do against another fighter's style. It would be fun to fight some of the bigger guys like Francis Ngannou, Stipe Miocic, or Ciryl Gane. At 185, a fight with Israel Adesanya would've been intriguing. I always tested myself and would've embraced the challenge against those guys. If you're not trying to fight killers, why are you even in the sport? My whole career was based off of fighting the best in the world.

I fought nineteen former world champions from the UFC, Pride, Strikeforce, and Bellator. My resume includes wins over the all-time greats. Fedor. Big Nog. Wanderlei. Vitor. Shogun. I fought guys who will never be forgotten. DC, Anderson Silva, Rampage. I have fights that will never be lost. Both Shogun fights, the Bisping KO, the Wanderlei KO, the Lombard KO, and the Fedor KO. When people talk about pound-for-pound or greatest of all time—I let fans decide that. There's some excellent newer-generation fighters like the Dagestanis. I was a fan of Khabib Nurmagomedov and his ability to make the fight go his way. He did a great job of doing that, which is a big part of winning a fight. Fighting your fight and not your opponent's. That area of the world has always been tough, dating back to my Soviet Union days. Now that style of Khabib, Islam Makhachev, and Khamzat Chimaev will thrive until there is someone who's an excellent wrestler and dangerous on the feet to mitigate their sambo and strengths.

Even though I am happily retired, my wife wants me to fight again. For her, it's the camaraderie and people that would come together for my fights. There's been a solid group of fifty people in my circle who would show up to my fights two to three times a year. Rachel would be able to hang out with them for about four days, and since I retired, it's rare we all get together. For my fiftieth birthday, most of them were able to come for my surprise party in Cabo, but it's definitely not the same. I do have an annual pig roast that brings a lot of them out of the woodwork, but as the years go by, things change a little more.

For the right price, I would come out of retirement. It would take $2 million for me to stop living a retired life to fight. I see the YouTubers drawing more eyes to boxing. Jake Paul has been choosing MMA fighters who don't have one-punch knockout power to hurt him. Someone asked me if I would fight Jake. If the price was right, not a problem. But I don't think Jake would want to fight somebody like me. If he beats me, he's beating an old man; if I win, it would be an embarrassment to him. But I guarantee you I'd beat his ass with my patented H-Bomb.

I also get the question, why didn't I fight my friend, Randy? We never entered the same tournaments because it really didn't make sense. But we would've fought each other. We kicked each other's asses in training almost every day for a handful of years for free, why wouldn't we do it for money? I know some BJJ guys get funny about fighting teammates, but as wrestlers, we just saw fights as competition.

It is cool to be recognized by people I would call celebrities. When my daughter was playing in a volleyball tournament in Arizona, Brett Favre was there and someone pointed him out to me. I doubted that he knew who I was, so I stayed in my seat. After some matches Brett walked up to me and said he was a fan of mine. I was shocked since the NFL is on a whole other level than MMA in the United States. But I've been around other football guys. I was at a table with my buddy, country star Chase Rice, when NFL star Travis Kelce came to me and said, "You're a fucking legend!" Over the years I've become friends with other country stars who followed my career, including Toby Keith, whose song, "Made In America," I walked out to the last ten years of my career. I have much more time now to travel the country and go to their shows.

I sometimes think, what would I have done if I didn't get into mixed martial arts? I would've probably been a chiropractor since I was accepted into a chiropractor school. If I didn't get a wrestling scholarship, I think the military would have been my number-one choice. I wouldn't have hesitated to put my life on the line for my country. I believe I would've been pretty good at it as well. I'm an outdoorsy guy and would have been proud to serve under any branch. There were times I would go visit the troops on various USO type tours, since I was and still am grateful for the soldiers putting their lives on the line for my freedom, which gave me options to make different choices in my life. I try and give back by doing as many events as possible for our troops.

I've been able to perfect my craft over a span of nearly six decades. The foundation is the same to every modality. *Confidence.* In a street fight, you need to go into it with not only some skills, but you need to eradicate fear. Fight or flight. If you think you're going to get your ass kicked, you probably are, so if there is a lack of confidence, you can run away, which isn't the worst thing in the world.

In mixed martial arts, a fighter must be confident in their abilities. They need to know they have to impose their will on their opponent. That all goes back to preparation. Did you do enough to have that confidence and mental fortitude? It all starts with mentality. If I didn't think I could win, I wouldn't set foot in the cage.

But you can apply this mentality and confidence to your own facets of life. Whether you want to work in clerical, as a firefighter, as a nurse, or in any other job, you need training for it to the best of your abilities. In turn, that will give you a newfound confidence when it is time to compete against someone for a job or to do the job well. There are numerous correlations you can make between life and fighting. Just because you don't get in a cage or ring doesn't mean you're not a fighter.

It is the life experiences and choices you make in your life that make you who you are. You become who you are by the people that guide you along your journey. That could be parents, coaches, teachers, friends, or mentors. Those will make a big difference in how you approach life and how you operate. I think I've made good decisions with the people who were around me. It started with my parents, and it was my dad who started my life's trajectory. It was because of him that I was able to achieve the things I did in wrestling and mixed martial arts. Bob helped cultivate my skills and mindset, which drove my mental toughness to levels I didn't know I had in me.

I know not everyone starts out at the same starting line in life, and I have been fortunate. But that doesn't mean you can't change. Surround yourself with solid individuals. The more good people you have around you, the better your decision-making will be. On the adverse, bad people may lead you to make not the greatest decisions.

I wasn't perfect growing up, still not today, but the older I got, the more my decision-making improved. I wasn't a bully; I disliked bullies, and didn't get in much trouble once I put my focus on wrestling. And the older I got, the better my group of friends became. I dropped off the bad ones along the way. I'm my own worst critic, but I know my dad and Bob are proud of me. They should be proud of themselves for their efforts as well. Bob was an old-school special breed of a coach. His methodology for coaching should be used more often. I don't see coaches today forcing their fighters to learn from others, but he did. He didn't have an ego like many coaches I see today. He welcomed experts to teach his proteges in areas where he didn't have all the answers. Bob retired from coaching and competing, but he definitely deserves a lot of credit for my accomplishments.

My dad has been on the decline. He was a warrior when I was growing up, but now he needs a weekly infusion due to the genetic autoimmune disorder alpha-1 antitrypsin. He was wrestling in the 1980 Olympic Trials and could not finish a match. He had shortness of breath, and all of his wind was gone. He didn't know what was wrong with him, and over the years, his health deteriorated. In 2017, he was finally diagnosed with alpha-1. The disease can cause damage to someone's lungs and liver—and in my father's case, he lost 80 percent of his lungs. His parents were of Scandinavian descent and both carriers, so it was passed on to him. I am a carrier of it as well, but since my mom's descendants were not of that region, it has bypassed me. The life expectancy of someone with alpha-1 is sixty years of age, but my dad is still around at seventy-four. What makes the disease even more disconcerting is that my dad was meticulously healthy growing up. He didn't smoke, worked out regularly, and had a healthy routine. That goes to show you that anything can happen to you at any moment or time. You shouldn't take life for granted.

On my mom's side, my grandmother was Native American and was born on an Indian reservation. I have a smidgen of Walla Walla Native in my blood; I definitely have the Native color and look but didn't know much about those roots until I got older. A few years back, I did go to the Walla Walla reservation and was able to do a sweat lodge with the chief in Oregon. Since I connected with those roots, I've gone back to do it a few times, and it's been interesting getting to know some of my ancestors' pasts who were warriors in their own right. Except in their case, those battles ended in bloodshed and death; I just took the death out of my occupation.

I get the post-retirement questions all the time. "Dan, what do you do now that your career is over?" It may seem like retired fighters' lives end. I know for many prizefighters, retirement hasn't been good to them. Many of the older boxers would get addicted to alcohol or substances. I've seen the stories of the Sugar Ray Robinsons, Rocky Marcianos, Sonny Listons, and Joe Louises once their careers came to a close. I understand that. No more walking into an arena with tens of thousands screaming fans. No more PPVs with millions watching you perform live on television. The lights fade. The chants dissipate. Next thing you know, you're at home and don't have to train on Monday. No more fight camp needed. There's no need for sparring partners anymore.

That can lead some to a downward spiral. Many fighters can't stand that feeling and go back to fighting when they shouldn't. It's sad to see the old, aged lion who was once king of the jungle get into the ring or cage and get knocked out. In February 2023, I saw Fedor's retirement fight against Ryan Bader. It didn't go well; Fedor was TKO'd in the first round. In Fedor's prime, the fight would've been a lot tougher for Bader. Those fight elements can be like a drug, and many times fighters stay in the sport too long. It's good when a fighter is in their prime, and terrible when time has passed you by. Even today I think I could still compete and beat